Worlds
in One
Country

Worlds in One Country

A brief survey of South African
writing – Nineteenth Century to 1994

Denis Hirson

First published by Jacana Media (Pty) Ltd in 2011

10 Orange Street
Sunnyside
Auckland Park 2092
South Africa
+2711 628 3200
www.jacana.co.za
Job No. 001565

© Denis Hirson, 2011

All rights reserved.

ISBN 978-1-4314-0247-2

Cover design Shawn Paikin and Maggie Davey
Set in Janson 11/16pt
Printed by Ultra Litho (Pty) Limited, Johannesburg

Cover picture:
Tondo drawing I, 2000
Charcoal on paper
130 x 122 cm
Courtesy Marian Goodman Gallery, New York and the artist

See a complete list of Jacana titles at www.jacana.co.za

CONTENTS

Preface vii

Acknowledgements xi

Worlds in One Country 1

Notes 101

Bibliography 123

Index 137

PREFACE

This text was written as an introduction to a book in French commissioned by the Institut français, cultural wing of the French Ministry of Foreign and European Affairs,[1] in the context of the planned 'seasons' of French culture in South Africa in 2012, and South African culture in France in 2013. That book includes essays by Denise Coussy and Joan Metelerkamp, respectively on South African prose and poetry since 1994, each essay followed by a mini-anthology. There is also a bibliography of work published in French, and a CD compilation of South African voices. As for the introduction, at the outset I swore to limit it to just a few pages, the intention being to simply create a context for what followed. But given the complexity of this context, my words started proliferating overnight, despite the fact that the information I wanted to include was, for the most part, highly abbreviated. What I have now done is to take that introduction and expand it so that it stands as a volume on its own.

Denis Hirson

It has been particularly challenging to try to gain an overview of South African writing, in all its forms, since its multiple beginnings. South Africans have for so long constrained themselves and been constrained within painfully, blindingly narrow boundaries, and their writing too has so often mirrored these delimitations. It is remarkable how few texts of South African fiction have ever given a sense of the writer being able to see simultaneously from the perspective of different groups, or individuals representing these groups. On the contrary, writers have devoted limitless verbal and emotional energy to the perceived walls of separation, attempting to either jump across them or build them even higher.

Likewise, those who have written about South African literature have often tended to look at one aspect of it: prose, poetry or theatre, black or white, in one language or another. I have tried to be as inclusive as possible here, taking advantage of my distance from the country since I live in France, and undertaking my task with a certain naivety I might not have had were I involved in the academic study of my subject. In fact, without this naivety, I doubt I would have undertaken the task at all, given the wealth of information I have had to sift through. The result is inevitably imperfect. Nor, given the historical development of South Africa, could it possibly have any semblance of wholeness. It is a strange patchwork, made of very different bits of cloth, from out of a badly torn, often violently ripped reality. It cannot be neatly sewn together. There are gaping holes, bits still flying in a raging wind, others that have no doubt entirely escaped me. Still, I have tried to take into account as much as possible. There will always be many other ways of doing so. In addition, this text goes only as far as 1994, due to the original brief for the introduction to the French book.

I have been guided by many works, and should express my indebtedness in particular to JM Coetzee's *White Writing*,[2] Nadine Gordimer's *The Black Interpreters*[3] and Njabulo S Ndebele's *Rediscovery of the Ordinary*,[4] as well as other critical work by these three writers.

I have also benefited enormously from the help of Robert Berold and Stephen Clingman, and wish to thank them for incisive comments, corrections and pointers in fresh directions. Thanks to Georges Lory for his advice, and Jeremy Hirson-Sagalyn for technical help. I wish to express my appreciation to the French Embassy in South Africa and particularly the ambassador M Jacques Lapouge for generously offering partial funding for this book, as well as to Georges Lory in his capacity as general director of the Alliances françaises of Southern Africa, and Jérôme Chevrier of the French Institute of South Africa, for giving it their full support.

Denis Hirson

I also wish to thank the book department of the Institut français in Paris, under the direction of Paul de Sinety, without whom this text, like the book it originally introduced, would never have seen the light of day. Lastly, I want to thank Nicolas Peccoud, also of the Institut français, whose meticulous, demanding reading of the introduction in French allowed me to clarify and extend it before proceeding with this publication in English.

ACKNOWLEDGEMENTS

For permission to quote from their own poems: Breyten Breytenbach, Jeremy Cronin, Ingrid de Kok, Antjie Krog, Oswald Mtshali, Karen Press, Lesego Rampolokeng, Mongane Wally Serote, Kelwyn Sole, Chris van Wyk, and John Irons, as translator of Eugène Marais.

For permission to quote from the poems of others: Jane Fox, for permission to quote from the work of Lionel Abrahams; NELM, for permission to quote from the work of Tatamkulu Afrika; Marjorie Clouts for permission to quote from the work of Sydney Clouts; Gregory Marsh as trustee of the Ingrid Jonker Trust, for permission to quote from the work of Ingrid Jonker; Deep South publishers for permission to quote from the work of Seitlhamo Motsapi; DALRO for permission to quote from the work of BWB Vilakazi.

Every effort has been made to contact other poets or those who hold their rights, for permission to publish their work. Unfortunately, we have not always been successful. If anyone has additional information, kindly notify the publisher.

Thanks to Bridget Impey of Jacana Media and Yamkela Khoza of the same as well as my agent Isobel Dixon for all their help, especially concerning permissions, during the final stages of the production of this book.

Last but not least: Thanks to William Kentridge and Anne McIlleron for help and permission to use the image on the front cover.

See the preface to this book for further acknowledgements.

WORLDS IN ONE COUNTRY

I began writing this text in 2010, in the midst of the soccer fever leading up to the FIFA World Cup. It was impossible to remain indifferent to this event since, quite apart from the burning question of who the eventual winner would be, it was of immense symbolic significance for South Africa to be hosting the World Cup in the first place. The year 2010 was a good one to be focussing on South Africa for other reasons, too. Since I wanted my text to combine literary and historical references, I could not help noticing how many other events came to mind that year, because the time was ripe to commemorate, or at least remember, their anniversaries.

The year 2010 was the hundredth anniversary of the declaration of the Union of South Africa, since in 1910 the white population reached a semblance of unity, born out of the blood of the South African (Anglo-

Boer) War. The British, in their drive to gain control of the recently discovered diamonds and gold in the two Boer Republics that constituted the interior of the country, had provoked a conflict that left more than 75 000 whites and blacks dead, vast tracts of farmland scorched, and barbed memories of the first ever concentration camps (set up by the British army) in the minds of the Boers. In 1910, the white Union, then populated by 4 million blacks, 500 000 coloureds, 150 000 Indians, and 1 275 000 whites, was declared a dominion of the British Empire.

The year 2010 was also the fiftieth anniversary of the Sharpeville massacre. This took place soon after whites began celebrating 50 years of union, a flurry of activity that built to a climax when the 'Flame of Civilisation', lit in Cape Town by the Governor-General Mr Swart, was carried through the streets of Johannesburg at the beginning of March 1960 during a parade of 6 000 people that included thousands of schoolchildren and many national sports players. On 21 March in Sharpeville, 5 000 unarmed blacks answered a call by the Pan Africanist Congress and gathered around the local police station to protest against the pass laws. More than 180 were wounded and 69 killed, almost all of them shot in the back by policemen under a bewildered officer who later commented that 'the Native mentality does not allow them to gather for a peaceful demonstration. For them to gather means violence'.[5]

The year 2010 brought back memories of unified, exclusive white rule and then the resurgence of a black political presence that could no more be acknowledged by the white regime than could the fact that by 1960 countries all over the continent were gaining their independence. And 2010 was equally the twentieth anniversary of the year when Nelson Mandela, one of the leaders who decided that political violence had indeed become necessary in the early 1960s, walked free after 27 years in prison. One week before his release, on 2 February 1990, the political parties that represented the majority of people in the country were finally legalised: the African National Congress (ANC), the Pan Africanist Congress (PAC) and the South African Communist Party (SACP), all of them long-banned (the latter in 1950, the other two in the wake of the Sharpeville massacre and the nationwide demonstrations that followed). The year 1990 was when teams led by Mandela and President FW de Klerk sat down at the negotiating table, deciding together on the future of South Africa, in which there was to be black political rule, even though a good portion of the wealth would remain in the hands of the then largely white ruling class and the overseas-controlled multinational corporations.

So 2010 was a year crowded with the potential reappearance of many contradictory historical moments, and yet the world was quite literally turning its eyes towards South Africa for very different reasons. For weeks, in a country where sport, like religion, had long been the occasion for fervent gatherings, teams bearing all the colours of the world went chasing a ball across 10 luxurious stadiums, in quest of the much-coveted World Cup. This event took place in a resolutely 'new' country of great multiracial crowd celebration, droning if not drowning among the vuvuzelas, while HIV/Aids, unemployment and housing problems stretched beyond the stadium walls.

And once again, during this event, history dovetailed with the present. The media highlighted the Makana Football Association (1966–1973), created by political prisoners on Robben Island, and named for the nineteenth-century Xhosa chief whose army of 18 000 stood up to colonial forces for several months, after which Makana was imprisoned on the Island, and drowned while trying to escape. And then there was the World Cup final itself, with the Dutch losing to Spain despite the support of a number of Afrikaners sporting the raw-carrot colours of their seventeenth-century ancestors.

❋

The World Cup had a specially intense flavour, not only for sports fans but for anyone who remembered that the idea of a South African team playing against opponents who were not white was, only three decades earlier, thought to be scandalously contemptuous in apartheid South Africa, while the idea of including a non-white player in their own team was simply unthinkable. For decades riots and boycotts surrounded South African teams whose shining pride at home was often seen as dark shame from abroad.

One person largely responsible for turning international opinion against South African sports teams (notably South Africa's exclusion from all Olympic Games for 28 years, beginning with Tokyo in 1964), was the coloured poet and activist Dennis Brutus, who was severely beaten as a prisoner on Robben Island for precisely this achievement, but who survived and later went into exile, and who died at the end of 2009.

'Through ceaseless countering of apartheid's deadliest weapon – its cultivation of ordinariness – Brutus engineered the gradual isolation that shattered the Nationalist fantasy of a civilised, law-abiding white outpost in Africa',[6] writes the poet Gabeba Baderoon, putting her finger on one reason why many writers under apartheid felt a strong need to take a political stand: an intolerably dehumanising system was in constant danger of being accepted as perfectly normal, from both inside and outside the country. The acceptance of oppressive ordinariness is a form of paralysis with a historically high incidence in South Africa, and resistance of one sort or another has been an integral part of the writer's role.

Under apartheid, writers and other artists, along with church leaders, raised their voices to fill the vacuum left by the absence of political leaders who were either in prison or exile, if they survived at all. But, more generally, writers have long used a political position as if it were an extra point marked upon the compass of their imagination, a means of orientation in this complex, fragmented society numbering 48.7 million people in 2011, with its multitude of cultures and traditions, ideological positions and official languages;[7] a way to root oneself, but also a rallying cry.

Here, for example, is a much-anthologised poem published in 1882 by the Reverend Isaac Wauchope, writing in Xhosa under the name of IWW Citashe:

> Your cattle are gone,
> My countrymen!
> Go rescue them! Go rescue them!
> Leave the breechloader alone
> And turn to the pen,
> Take paper and ink,
> For that is your shield.

Your rights are going!
So pick up your pen,
Load it, load it with ink,
Sit in your chair –
Repair not to Hoho,
But fire with your pen.[8]

Wauchope was one of a small and privileged missionary-educated group of Africans who had emerged by the 1870s, and had become convinced of the futility of continuing to take up arms against white settlers. Using both English and African languages (first transcribed by the missionaries themselves), members of this group turned to writing, and in the mid 1880s began establishing magazines and newspapers of their own. The most prominent of these was *Imvo Zabantsundu* (African Opinion), started by John Tengo Jabavu in King William's Town in 1884.

Significantly, this town is in the Eastern Cape, the region where missionaries accompanying British colonial forces had first settled and begun working among the predominantly Xhosa people. The first generation of African intellectuals was steeped in the Christian tradition. The 1866 Xhosa translation of Bunyan's *The Pilgrim's Progress*, by South Africa's first ordained black minister Tiyo Soga,[9] was 'almost as great an influence on the Xhosa language as the

Authorised Version of the Bible upon English', according to writer and academic AC Jordan.[10]

The next generation was already affirming a stronger African identity. Writers sometimes sought out the intersection between contemporary issues and inspiring historical subjects, as did Thomas Mofolo, of the French Morija Mission in Basutoland (Lesotho). He began working on his Sotho novel *Chaka* (completed in 1910, and published in 1925) about the nation-building but also morally destructive ambitions of the powerful Zulu king, soon after the 1906 Bambatha Rebellion. (The Zulu chief Bambatha led a rebellion against the imposition of a poll tax on his tribesmen and 4 000 of his men lost their lives during the ruthless repression that followed, with Bambatha himself being decapitated. This rebellion is today regarded by some historians as the beginning of the struggle against white rule in South Africa.) Mofolo's Chaka, in order to become the greatest of all chiefs, gives in to the demands of the diviner Isanusi, killing his own mistress, Noliwe, and – according to Mofolo – finally his own mother, Nandi. Mofolo presents Chaka's neurotic bloodlust as symbolic of the paroxysm of a dying nation. When at the end of the book the spears of his assassins meet in his body, he says: 'You are killing me in the hope that you will be kings when I am dead, whereas you are wrong, that is not the way it will be because *umlungu*, the white man, is coming, and it is he who will rule you, and you will be his servants.'[11]

Another writer, Sol Plaatje, once again mission-educated, actively Christian but also first General Secretary of the South African Native National Congress (SANNC), which would later become the African National Congress (ANC), bridged the gap between journalism and book-length testimony in his *Boer War Diary* (1901),[12] as well as the landmark survey *Native Life in South Africa* (1916). This book starts out as a protest against the 1913 Native Land Act, which reduced possible black ownership to seven per cent of the land, and led Plaatje to open his first chapter with the statement that 'Awaking on Friday morning, June 20, 1913, the South African native found himself, not actually a slave, but a pariah in the land of his birth.'[13] Among other achievements, Plaatje translated Shakespeare into his native Setswana, not simply to make high culture available, but also to demonstrate the capacity of an African language to express all that was assumed to be the special province of English.[14] By 1920, Plaatje had completed the first black novel in English, *Mhudi*,[15] telling the story of an 1830 war caused by the burden of a tax imposed by the Matabele under Mzilikazi on the Baralong, who entered an alliance with the Boers. During this war Mhudi, a brave Barolong woman, goes to bring her wounded future husband Ra-Thaga back from the front. Like Mofolo's *Chaka*, *Mhudi* affirms an African identity, rooted in tradition, while Christian ideas and the violent process of white colonisation are woven into the story. Both books can be read to imply a protest about current events, *Chaka* with reference to the Bambatha Rebellion and *Mhudi* pointing to the Land Act. 'What happened in the 1830s might happen in the twentieth century, only to different oppressors. Plaatje is sounding an implicit warning: he is not advocating revolution – merely indicating its inevitability if certain conditions prevail.'[16]

In the 1920s, less than 10 per cent of the black population was literate, so that the readership of writers such as Plaatje and his predecessors was restricted to the elite. Plaatje writes in sophisticated and at times ornate English, and clearly has an overseas readership in mind when he writes such sequences as 'Passing a miniature lake – called a pan in South Africa – filled with the waters of the recent flood, Mhudi paused to admire a flock of wild ducks swimming gracefully on the still water'.[17] Yet *Mhudi*, like *Chaka*, is strongly influenced by the oral tradition of storytelling and oral poetry, which at the same time precede and lie at the heart of early black South African writing. This is also the case for AC Jordan's novel *Ingqumbo Yeminyana* (*The Wrath of the Ancestors*, 1940),[18] originally written in

Xhosa. A young prince, Zwelinzima, reluctantly leaves the black University College of Fort Hare to return to his ancestral home and take his place as king of his people. But his modern ideas are unacceptable there, and his reign ends with his suicide as well as that of his wife Nobantu and their child. An ancient world of royalty, priests and councillors, with their customs and formal manner of address, plays out its tragic drama in a world filled with motorcars, cricket players, newspapers and schools.

The same influence of the oral tradition can still be felt today, as has been demonstrated by the presence of *iimbongi* at Nelson Mandela's inauguration and many other ceremonial events. *Iimbongi* function as both praise-singers and political commentators, combining a rich use of metaphor, hallucinatory rhythm, political and historical knowledge, and a sharp sense of occasion. The first of them to successfully exploit the new medium of print, in Xhosa works such as *Imihobe Nemibongo* (Joyous Songs and Lullabies, 1927),[19] was SEK Mqhayi, who also composed most of the lyrics for what has become the national anthem, 'Nkosi Sikelel' i Afrika'.[20] There is an account of Nelson Mandela as a young student witnessing an impressive performance by Mqhayi at his high school, reciting 'his well-known poem about the division of the stars, gesturing to the skies with his assegai'.[21] Here is part of the poem:

> You Sotho,
> Take Canopus,
> To share with the Tswana and Chopi,
> And all of those nations in loincloths.
> You of KwaZulu,
> Take Orion's Belt,
> To share with the Swazi, the Chopi and Shangaan,
> As well as uncircumcised nations.
> You Britons, take Venus,
> To divide with the Germans and Boers,
> Though you're folk who don't know how to share.
> We'll divide up the Pleiades, we people of Phalo,
> For they're stars for counting off years,
> For counting the years of manhood,
> For counting the years of manhood [...][22]

Here is Mqhayi again, this time directly addressing the Prince of Wales in 1925:

> She sent us the preacher, she sent us the bottle,
> She sent us the Bible, and barrels of brandy,
> She sent us the breechloader, she sent us cannon;
> O, roaring Britain! Which must we embrace?
>
> You sent us the truth, denied us the truth,
> You sent us the life, deprived us of life,
> You sent us the light, we sit in the dark,

Shivering, benighted in the bright noonday sun.[23]

Plaatje's *Mhudi* was in fact published in 1930, two years after RRR Dhlomo's novella *An African Tragedy*,[24] which relates the questionable moral behaviour of a man who goes to Johannesburg to seek work, as well as the sordid conditions he encounters in the slums. Dhlomo, who went on to write historical novels about the lives and times of nineteenth-century Zulu kings, also wrote short urban stories such as 'The Dog Killers', about the killing, ordered by the white administration, of all dogs owned by blacks in a mining compound. Saturated with violence, this story ends with the image of one miner, Jama, 'his face swollen, disfigured, clotted with blood ... dead! And just close to his right hand lay his dog, Boy, with its body mangled out of shape ...'.[25] Such fiction marks the shift in location of black writing to the city (just as a parallel shift was occurring in white writing). The backdrop to the migration recorded by writers such as Dhlomo are the Natal poll tax (1905), the Land Act, and other laws severely restricting if not suffocating the capacity of blacks to earn a livelihood in the countryside. This obliged adults of working age and men in the first instance to migrate to the city, swelling the pool of cheap labour for whites, not least of all in the labour-intensive mines. I will return below to the significant body of literature that responds to this situation.

❋

The beginnings of white writing in South Africa can be traced back to travellers such as William J Burchell, an English botanist, ornithologist, anthropologist and natural historian whose *Travels in the Interior of Southern Africa* (1822)[26] records his impressions during his stay from 1811 to 1813, and his disappointment that this landscape is inferior to the English one, lacking for instance in the rich green colour he was so used to. JM Coetzee, discussing the English poets who tried to describe this landscape well into the twentieth century much as Burchell did, refers to 'a self-defeating process of naming Africa by defining it as non-Europe – self-defeating because in each particular in which Africa is identified to be non-European, it remains Europe, not Africa, that is named'.[27]

Over the decades Burchell was followed by many other travellers, as well as a number of British writers such as Rider Haggard, who stayed for periods in South Africa itself, setting his colourful adventures there and elsewhere in Africa. His black characters are noble and fierce yet subservient savages, who nonetheless – regrettably, as far as Haggard is concerned – call into question a long history of European representation of Africa, as in this extract from *Allan Quatermain* (1887): 'I say that as the savage is, so is the white man, only the latter is more inventive, and possesses the faculty of combination; save and except also that the savage, as I have known him, is to a large extent free from the greed of money, which eats like a cancer into the heart of the white man. It is a depressing conclusion, but in all essentials the savage and the child of civilization are identical.'[28]

Among the approximately 5 000 British settlers who arrived in the Cape Colony in 1820 was the Scotsman Thomas Pringle, a Romantic writer who was soon editing two newspapers, the *South African Journal* and the *South African Commercial Advertiser*, both of them eventually suppressed for their open criticism of the colonial government. Before being hounded from the Cape by the English Governor, Pringle recorded his impressions of the South African people and landscapes in both prose and awkward, archaic poetry, again making his political position known. The poem 'The Caffer Commando' includes the lines 'For England hath spoken in her tyrannous mood/ And the edict is writing in African blood!'[29] *Narrative of a Residence in South Africa*,[30] published in 1834, is written by someone who, despite his nationality, considered South Africa to be his home, travelling to places few foreigners had visited, expressing a feeling of deep sympathy for local people. Also in 1834, Pringle – now back in England and working as Secretary to the Anti-Slavery Society – was instrumental in getting the Reformed British parliament to pass legislation bringing an end to slavery in the British dominions.

The abolition of slavery in the Cape led to more than 7 000 families of Dutch and Huguenot origin leaving the Cape in ox-wagons over the following five or six years, taking with them their slaves and their cattle, and ultimately colonising the land that comprised two Boer Republics, the Zuid-Afrikaansche Republiek of the Transvaal, and the Orange Free State (with reference to the Dutch House of Orange). Behind them they left not only the Cape Colony, but the strict policy of the Cape administration that Dutch should be spoken by all, including slaves.[31] In the interior of the country, the trekkers became farmers. By the 1850s their language, Afrikaans – of mainly Dutch origin but including elements of other languages such as the 'Malay' spoken by some of the first slaves at the Cape, as well as African languages and Portuguese – was being written down in newspapers and political and religious works. After diamonds and then gold had been discovered on their territory, in 1867 and 1886 respectively, they lost the South African War of 1899–1902 to the British. One man who was instrumental in this defeat was Sir Percy FitzPatrick, editor of the *Barberton Gold Fields News*, transport rider, tried for high treason for his part in the abortive Jameson Raid that aimed to destabilise the Transvaal Boer republic, co-founder of the Imperial Light Horse Regiment and later South African Member of Parliament. FitzPatrick's best-selling autobiographical book of veld adventures with his Staffordshire Bull Terrier, *Jock of the Bushveld* (1907)[32] has so far been through 91 editions and impressions. Adventure was a key element of books about the South African War itself. Along with the Great Trek, it has been the subject of epic, myth-making fictional accounts by writers such as Rayn Kruger, Arthur Conan Doyle and Stuart Cloete. Unlike a book such as Deneys Reitz's autobiographical narrative, *Commando: A Boer Journal of the Boer War*[33] (which has the freshness and fine detail of an account written immediately after the war), many accounts of both these events by Afrikaners have an undertone of deep grievance against the British. They also often reveal the sense of a mystical bond between their lineage and the land.[34]

In 1883 an English-speaking writer, Olive Schreiner, daughter of a Lutheran missionary writing under the pseudonym of Ralph Iron, published *The Story of an African Farm*,[35] the first South African novel to achieve strong international acclaim. The book hinges on the fate of the relentlessly freethinking Lyndall, an orphan who grows up alongside her conventional, accommodating cousin Em. Lyndall (also the maiden name of Schreiner's mother) seeks a way out of both the barren confines of white frontier society, and the oppressive fate awaiting her as a woman.[36] 'I like to realise forms of life utterly unlike mine,' she says, imagining a sensual world that includes among others a mediaeval monk, little naked Malay boys, a Hindu philosopher, a troop of Bacchanalians and a black 'witchdoctor'. 'I like to see it all [...], it breaks down the narrow walls that shut me in.'[37]

Schreiner is didactically forthright in her feminist, atheist views. Her 'African farm' lacks a substantial material existence, the sheep that form the basis of its economy are barely present, the black labourers little more than extras.[38] Yet the novel is alive with believable and at times strangely funny characters, all the way from the fat, man-devouring Afrikaner farm-woman, to Lyndall's spurned husband, who eventually disguises himself as a female nurse so that he can tend to her on her deathbed. In telling their story, Schreiner also becomes the first South African writer to render the South African landscape in a novel: 'The plain was a weary flat of loose red sand sparsely covered by dry karroo bushes, that cracked beneath the tread like tinder, [...] the red walls of the farmhouse, the zinc roofs of the outbuildings, the stone walls of the "kraals", all reflected the fierce sunlight, till the eye ached and blenched. No tree or shrub was to be seen far or near.'[39]

Later, in the 1920s and '30s, at about the same time as Afrikaans became one of the country's two official languages along with English (in 1925), the first truly home-grown white South African literary genre was born. This was the *plaasroman* (farm novel),[40] as developed in Afrikaans by CM van den Heever and others. Writing in the wake of the major drought and depression that hit farming communities (the 1931 Carnegie Commission on poor whites concluded that more than one third of Afrikaners lived as paupers), they rejected the perceived corrupting life of the city and its material attractions, seen as a threat to the Afrikaner's economic independence and cultural identity. Instead, they idealised a strongly feudal version of farm life where, as on Schreiner's farm, the human presence of the black labour force was barely recognised. The *plaasroman* also found an echo in the work of English-speaking writer Pauline Smith, who wrote a series of short stories, some of them collected together in *The Little Karoo* (1925). Here, in the face of a dying rural order, she created a kind of Old Testament Eden; a place of refuge but also of virtuous suffering and sacrifice. For example, the young Niccoline Johanna in 'The Pastor's Daughter' is caught in a moral dilemma over the man she wishes to marry: 'My mother said at last: "My child, when I am dead and you are with Paul Marais in the Transvaal how will it go with your pa? Your pa is a saint, but like all the saints he is also a fool. When I am dead and you are with Paul in the Transvaal, how will it go with him?"'[41]

Among the last of the *plaasroman* novels was *Huisies teen die Heuwel* (*Houses on the Hillside*, 1942)[42] by CH Kühn, writing under the pseudonym of Mikro. Here, the son of respectable coloured farm workers, recently released from jail, returns to the farm and attempts to subvert his fellows with 'communist' ideas. But he is killed in a brawl, and the farmer concludes that he must punish his workers in the same way as a father might deal with his lazy children.

Parallel to the development of the *plaasroman*, there was a renewal in the field of Afrikaans poetry. This had begun in the first decades of the century with 'Die Taalstryd', the struggle for the official recognition of the Afrikaans language itself, in the wake of the South African War. Among the writers instrumental in this movement were Jan FE Celliers, C Louis Leipoldt, Totius (JD du Toit), CJ Langenhoven (author in 1918 of the poem 'Die Stem' [The Voice], later put to music to become the Afrikaans version of the national anthem) and Eugène N Marais. Marais, owner at an early age of the newspaper *Land en Volk* (Land and [Afrikaner] People), was best known as a pioneering ethologist whose book *The Soul of the White Ant* (1925)[43] was replicated if not plagiarised by Nobel prize-winner Maurice Maeterlinck. His poem 'Winter Night' (often pointed to as proof that a literary aesthetic was possible in Afrikaans) can be taken as indicative of the mood of desolation following the South African War, the last line of this quote possibly referring to the British destruction of Boer farms:

> So cold now the wind is
> and spare.
> And bleak in the dim light
> and bare,
> as wide as God's mercy and boundless,
> the scorched veld lies starlit and soundless.[44]

A generation later came playwright and poet NP van Wyk Louw, co-founder of the literary magazine *Standpunte* (Viewpoints) and leading light of the Dertigers (Writers of the Thirties) movement, producing a body of work extremely wide in its range and ambition (like that of the poet considered to be his successor, DJ Opperman, it was showered with Afrikaans-language literary prizes). Louw's choric drama *Die Dieper Reg* (The Greater Right),[45] written for the centenary of the Great Trek, is set in the Hall of Eternal Righteousness, where the Voortrekkers have come after death to face the Prosecutor who will judge their deeds. In a song addressed to the country of South Africa itself, a 'wide and woeful land, alone/ under the great southern stars', the trekkers are presented as

> Simple people who perform
> true and singly bitter things
> and singly fall like grains of seed;
> dumb deeds, small trust, small treachery
> of those who for another lord
> like serfs leave you in need.[46]

If the heavy aesthetic of such language was ultimately employed to justify white nationalism, Louw nonetheless found himself at odds with National Party politics. In a key 1936 essay, 'Die rigting van die Afrikaanse letterkunde' (The direction of Afrikaans literature), he stated that 'everything, absolutely everything that moves the modern person, which forms his joy or his sorrow, must find expression in our literature'.[47] Louw's own intimate poetry is stripped of the defensiveness of his political work. In 'Ballad of the

Night Hours' the poet finds himself despairing after a woman at a party, whose 'crooked paper hat/ glided far away in the dance hall'. He concludes:

> And now the morning has spilt me
> Over the rim of its glass
> On the verandah near the shiny tap
> In the hour of the dark thirst. [48]

By the 1920s, there were already early examples of a new theme being developed in white writing, parallel to RRR Dhlomo's *An African Tragedy*: stories recounting the fate of black migrants travelling to the white city. Among the first of these was a short story by William Plomer, 'Ula Masondo' (1927), in which a black migrant worker, having narrowly escaped death in the mines, returns home to Zululand and rejects his own mother. '"Who are you? Leave me alone," he said, "you bloody heathen."'[49] Soon after this incident the mother hangs herself.

Plomer's first novel, *Turbott Wolfe* (1926),[50] published in England by Virginia and Leonard Woolf's Hogarth Press, concerns the unresolved, unconsummated relationship between the eponymous young Englishman and Nhliziyombi, a black customer at his trading store in Zululand. In response to the prevailing bigotry, Wolfe is involved in starting a political association, Young Africa, which promotes the idea that interracial sex will lay the foundations for the future 'Coloured World'. The association implodes, and Wolfe ends up leaving the country. Yet the philosophical position underpinning this story, for which its author found little support, announces that 'the colonial cord is ruptured, early on and for ever, for South African literature because Plomer's novel does not measure Africa against the white man, but the white man against Africa'.[51] Plomer himself left South Africa in 1926, but beforehand did meet up with two writers of like mind. The first of these was Roy Campbell, best known for his acidly satirical, highly colourful poetry, his ultimately reactionary position during the Spanish Civil War, and well before that his damning of blandly repressive colonial culture, as in his famous four-lined poem 'On Some South African Novelists':

> You praise the firm restraint with which
>   they write –
> I'm with you there, of course:
> They use the snaffle and the curb all right,
> But where's the bloody horse?[52]

The third writer was the novelist and explorer Laurens van der Post, who like Plomer held to the conviction that the future of the country was neither white nor black, but brown, though his early work explored the extreme difficulty of black-white relations. In *In a Province* (1934) the liberal Johan van Bredepoel fails despite all his good intentions to help Kenon Badiakgotla, a young man who has left his kraal for the fictional town of Port Benjamin and has been caught up in a world of crime. "'Ah,' he thought, "we were brothers in misfortune and inadaptability, but I could have helped him, and I didn't. Remote from one another we passed through life like two shadows over a hill, darkening it, but not altering it. Our lives were set in a corridor shut at both ends.'"[53]

Van der Post was to become famous for his books about the Japanese during the Second World War, as well as the first southern African people, the San, or / Xam (*The Lost World of the Kalahari*, 1958).[54] These people became part of his personal quest to discover the 'lost soul' of humankind, among people still alive in the Kalahari who were deeply connected with nature and the cosmos.

Decades earlier, in 1926, Van der Post, Plomer and Campbell briefly worked on the periodical *Voorslag* (Whiplash), questioning the colonial ethos of the time. All three withdrew after publication of the first few issues, angered by attempts to muzzle their writing.

It is interesting to set *Turbott Wolfe* side by side with a novel published just two years earlier, Sarah Gertrude Millin's *God's Stepchildren* (1924),[55] in which the author attempts to show how South African morality, based on colour, brings misery in its wake, but at the same time presents black blood as a 'flaw' that can be traced back through several generations of a white family. A white missionary sinks into squalor and madness, obsessed with the 'sin' of having begotten half-caste children with a Khoi ('Hottentot') woman. The grandson, Barry Lindsell, unable to live with this birthright, finally reveals the secret to his young English wife, who is both surprised and relieved that nothing worse has been torturing his spirit. Millin, one of South Africa's most celebrated writers in her heyday, produced 17 novels, including the bestselling *King of the Bastards* (1949),[56] which clearly shows her right-wing political leanings: a white community is 'polluted' by black blood, and expels the defiler in terms of an edict that echoes the new apartheid government's race laws.

In the 1930s and '40s, blacks and whites made their way to the cities in ever-growing numbers. There were several reasons for this. The countryside had been hard hit by drought and depression; in addition, more blacks sought urban employment when the 1936 Native Trust and Land Act restricted their ownership to 13 per cent of all land in South Africa. 'Yes, we fold up our knees/ It's impossible to stretch out,/ Because the land has been hedged in,' wrote the Xhosa poet St J Page Yako.[57] Lastly, jobs left behind by soldiers fighting in the Second World War were filled by both white women and blacks. By 1946, one year after the war had ended, blacks in the Witwatersrand numbered half a million; by 1959, 50 000 more had entered the region, despite severe influx control.

In 1948 the National Party was elected to power on a wave of Afrikaner populism rising out of the depression years. New legislation, inspired by the Nazi sympathisers who formed the core of the new government, crystallised centuries of racism. The fast-changing, fraught social atmosphere of a city like Johannesburg seemed to promise a strange new freedom from conservative rural communities, both black and white, but the city was also the scene of severe racial repression heightened by the policies of apartheid, and sharply set wealth and poverty side by side. The Zulu poet BWB Vilakazi talks of mineworkers being herded together before mine-dumps that rise up and 'blot out the world', feeling that

> Our family pride is gone, we are children,
> The world is clearly turned head over heels.
> Wakened up at dawn, stood in a row!
> Where have you known of a man once buried
> Who sees with both eyes open and stands alive?

Later in the same long poem, Vilakazi comments on how the mines bring to mind

> Wealth and the wealthy whom I made rich
> Climbing to the rooms of plenty, while I stay
> Squeezed of juice like flesh of a dead ox. [58]

The film *Jim Comes to Joburg*[59] shows a black man leaving his home in the country only to be mugged by black gangsters on arrival in the city, becoming a catastrophic suburban gardener and then achieving a measure of success as a nightclub singer. The film gave its name to a whole literary genre, of which the most renowned example is Alan Paton's *Cry, the Beloved Country* (1944).[60] In a story notable both for its religious undercurrent and the paternalistic portrayal of its black characters, the Reverend Stephen Kumalo travels from rural Natal to discover that his sister has become a prostitute in the city, while his son has killed a white man actively sympathetic towards the black cause. Kumalo, on returning home at the end of the story, is still a man of faith despite his shaken spirit. But as an agricultural expert tells him, the land is so eroded that it can no longer sustain his people. This, coupled with the archaism of the Zulu-speaking black characters,[61] signals the waning of an old black tribal world, economically as well as socially. Paton also foresees future black corruption and a polarised social situation, the Reverend Msimangu stating his fear regarding the whites 'that one day when they are turned to loving, they will find we are turned to hating'.[62] In some of his later works Paton confronts white violence more directly, as in the terse short story 'Life for a Life', where a coloured woman loses her husband in the feudal, revenge-driven atmosphere of an Afrikaner farm, later leaving for a life she hopes will be easier in the Cape.[6] Restlessness, uprooting and political friction characterise much of the white and black writing of this period.

Phyllis Altman's *The Law of the Vultures* (1952) follows the paths of two black men from the naivety of the countryside to the attractive, confusing world of Johannesburg, which ultimately becomes a 'blind world'[64] of humiliation and loss. Thabo Thaele has proudly become a clerk in an office, while David Nkosi, decorated for heroism as a soldier in Egypt (though like others of his colour he was not allowed to bear arms), arrives in the city to seek material compensation, which the army had promised but will not give him. Both, despite themselves, are finally confronted with a choice between violent anti-white action and tempered non-racial politics, including trade-unionism. In Harry Bloom's *Transvaal Episode* (1955)[65] the inhabitants of a township join together in a cataclysmic revolt against their white administrator Du Toit, a weak and initially well-meaning man who comes to realise when the violence has subsided that the police themselves are perpetrating inhuman crimes.

Modikwe Dikobe's novel *The Marabi Dance* (published in 1973 but written earlier) describes Johannesburg, beginning in the 1930s, as seen from a city slum yard where the main character, Martha, is caught between a tribal past she has never known and tumultuous, squalid life in the city. In her quest for romance she must dodge characters such as the sexually voracious Bitch-Never-Die, the leader of the Black Cat gang who 'could not finish a sentence in a single language',[66] and the tragicomic, bogus 'Reverend' Ndlovu, trying to take advantage of those lost in this transitional world. Peter Abrahams sets *Mine Boy* (1946) in precisely the same context, one that 'makes you strange to the world of your people'.[67] From out of a swirl of women and alcohol, Xuma,[68] newly arrived from the countryside, makes his way to the mines where he ultimately leads a strike in protest against perilous conditions underground. This is the first full novel in which the city is seen through the eyes of a black worker.

Much black writing of the 1950s and early 1960s is autobiographical testimony: Peter Abrahams' *Tell Freedom* (1954),[69] Ezekiel (later Es'kia) Mphahlele's *Down Second Avenue* (1959),[70] Bloke Modisane's *Blame Me on History* (1963).[71] Such works are made out of the precise details of poverty and daily violence, the harsh and humiliating experience of racial discrimination, the energies needed to overcome what Mphahlele names as 'a fatally beautiful lady called bitterness'.[72] Each of these writers has contact with benevolent or politically radical whites; each is tempted by political engagement, followed by disillusionment and ultimately exile, in turn leading to constant writing about the unresolved situation that has been left behind and remains the pivot of the imagination.

Thematically, as Mphahlele points out, the writing of this time centres again and again on the crucial yet limiting question of race relations: 'The main weakness in South African writers is that they are hyperconscious of the race problem in their country. They are so obsessed with the subject of race and colour that when they set about writing creatively they imagine that the plot they are going to devise, the characters they are going to create and the setting they are going to exploit, must subserve an important message or important discovery they think they have made in race relations.'[73]

Despite his reservations, since he wanted above all to teach and write fiction, escaping what he retrospectively termed the 'crushing cliché'[74] of apartheid, Mphahlele joined the staff of *Drum* magazine, founded in the early 1950s and directed above all at an urban black readership. There he was joined by some of the most talented writers of the time, including Henry 'Mr Drum' Nxumalo, Bloke Modisane, Arthur Maimane, Casey Motsitsi, Nat Nakasa, Lewis Nkosi and Can Themba. Among the flashy cover-girl pictures and pages devoted to muckraking and entertainment, they interspersed stories and serious articles, giving voice to the urban experience with the descriptive immediacy of American B-movies and local street language at a time when blacks in the white city were expected to be as silent and invisible as servants at a banquet.

Although lacking in political depth, *Drum* also covered the significant events of the decade, including the adoption of the Freedom Charter (gathering together various multiracial opposition parties of the Congress Alliance and signed in 1953); the Treason Trial (in which 156 opposition leaders were charged with high treason in 1956) and the Sharpeville massacre

(1960). *Drum* staff, characterised by a certain bravado, challenged prevailing norms, as when Bloke Modisane, sent to 'test the validity of Christian brotherhood', had himself 'bodily thrown into the den of white Christian lions' and then promptly thrown out again, as he was forcibly expelled from an all-white church service.[75] 'A *Drum* man,' according to Lewis Nkosi, '[…] was supposed to exhibit a unique intellectual style, usually urbane, ironic, morally tough and detached […] especially in reporting the uncertainties of urban African life in the face of rigorous apartheid laws. Above all, in *Drum* […] one couldn't deal professionally with urban African life unless one had descended to its very depths as well as climbed to its heights. A *Drum* man took sex and alcohol in his stride, or was supposed to, and stayed in the front line of danger.'[76]

This 'urban African life' was not uniquely black. *Drum*'s early years corresponded to a period of intense multiracial collaboration among a small minority of people, not only in the political arena, but also in the world of theatre and music. During what Lewis Nkosi referred to as 'the fabulous decade',[77] blacks and whites, forbidden by law from sharing a drink, let alone any form of intimacy, dizzily flaunted these barriers during suburban parties, despite the constant threat of police raids. Nadine Gordimer was both witness to and participant in such events. She had already established her reputation with her first collection of short stories *Face to Face* (1949)[78] and her first novel *The Lying Days* (1953),[79] which explored a white girl's coming of age. In 1958 she published *A World of Strangers*,[80] recounting the story of a young Englishman, Toby Hood, in South Africa to work for the family business, who was not without resemblance to *Drum* editor Anthony Sampson. Hood moves between his affair with a divorcee in the wealthy white suburbs, and friendship with a dashing young black man, Steven Sitole, keeping his involvement in these deeply split worlds secretive until Sitole is killed in a car crash, after escaping from a club during a police raid.

Though Lewis Nkosi survived this time to become both a novelist and literary critic of note, by the end of the 1950s most *Drum* writers had either died or were in exile. Nat Nakasa committed suicide in New York. Henry Nxumalo was murdered after publishing many penetrating exposés, such as that of near-slave conditions endured by farm labourers on the Bethal potato farms, and another on the humiliation of black prisoners at the Fort in central Johannesburg. Can Themba, rich in talent as a writer of fiction and reportage, died of alcoholism in Swaziland. His short-story collection *The Will to Die* (1972) included 'The Suit', which told of jealousy and extreme humiliation between the members of a young Sophiatown couple, and was later to become a well-known play.[81] By the early 1960s, the mainly black residential area of Sophiatown, exceptionally a part of Johannesburg and often referred to in *Drum*, had been razed to the ground, only to be replaced by an Afrikaner suburb named Triomf (Triumph).

In *A Walk in the Night* (1962),[82] a novella by Alex La Guma (another *Drum* contributor), the main character Michael Adonis, a resident of District Six, the then multiracial area of Cape Town, loses his job and is confronted with the policy of job-reservation that favoured white employment. He accidentally kills a down-and-out white vagrant, then betrays a good friend and joins a gang. The implosive violence of a nonetheless finely written text is an indication of the state of black prose by the 1960s, years marked by the suffocating weight of repression.

If the black writing of the 1950s and early 1960s showed exceptional promise, it was followed by a drought of silence inside the country that lasted for a decade or more. In the early 1970s, Nadine Gordimer expressed the belief that 'a certain connection has been axed between black fiction writers and their material. Aspirant writers are intimidated not only by censorship as such but also by the fear that anything at all controversial, set out by a black in the generally explicit medium of prose, makes the writer suspect, since the correlation of articulacy and political insurrection, so far as blacks are concerned, is firmly lodged in the minds of the Ministers of the Interior, Justice and Police. Polymorphous fear cramps the hand.'[83]

Some white writing of the early 1950s reveals the position of a self-confronting narrator in the face of an alienating social environment. The Afrikaner playwright, publisher and translator Bartho Smit seemed to be looking through a crack in time when, in his prophetic short story 'I Take Back My Country', 1951 – first published in Afrikaans as 'Ek Vat My Land' in the popular magazine *Huisgenoot* – he has the white narrator say, 'Perhaps it was my conviction – which was also a profound fear – that the cultural future of this country lies locked in the hearts of the black millions and not in us.'[84] By the end of the story, this same narrator, after encountering a black painter intent on representing and reclaiming the untamed land, stumbles 'over the soil of a country where I was just one of a few homeless and unwanted guests'.[85]

In Dan Jacobson's novella *A Dance in the Sun* (1955),[86] two young hitchhikers who stop for the night in a desolate Karoo farm find themselves deeply disoriented as they bear witness to the harrowing violence that binds the farmer to his workers. In the short story 'The Zulu and the Zeide',[87] Jacobson describes the bond linking an old Jewish immigrant who is fast losing his clarity of mind to a young Zulu servant, like him a new immigrant to the city. Immigration is a theme Jacobson returns to in the multifaceted novel *The Beginners* (1966),[88] where the theme of footloose identity runs through three generations of a Jewish family. In an insightful essay on his hometown, Kimberley, he writes of 'this undescribed and uncertified place where not a single thing, from the sand underfoot to the occasional savage thunderstorm overhead, was as other places were. Everything around us was without confirmation, without background, without credentials; there was something unreliable, left out, about the whole place, and hence about all of us, too.'[89]

On the other hand, it was the certainty of rootedness characteristic of the Afrikaner farming community of the Marico bushveld, in the northwest of the country, that provided Herman Charles Bosman (born into an Afrikaans-speaking family yet writing in English) with material for some of South Africa's best-loved tales. Bosman's work, threaded with themes of jealousy, hatred, love and betrayal, manages to be both compassionate and sharply critical of the people it describes. Some of his stories reach the heart of wider political issues that confront a deeply rooted rural community. In 'Unto Dust' (1950), for example, the local inhabitants come to realise that the bones of a black man and a white man, both of them killed in the same colonial battle, have probably been accidentally mixed together, since the black man's faithful dog refuses to leave the white man's graveside. They are forced to admit that 'alive, you couldn't go wrong in distinguishing between a white man and a kafir. Dead, you had great difficulty in telling them apart.'[90] Bosman's irony often turned to laughter. In 'A Bekkersdal Marathon' (1950),[91] a congregation sings all 176 verses of Psalm 119, because the predikant goes into a trance before telling them when to stop. His fellow church elders and the organist fuel themselves secretly with alcohol to sustain the marathon, until the predikant emerges from his trance and asks them to start all over again.

Bosman, imprisoned and initially sentenced to death after fatally shooting his stepbrother during an argument, wrote one of the first South African autobiographical prison narratives, *Cold Stone Jug* (1949).[92] Filled with light humour that dispels the darkness, Bosman's detailed account does not neglect the sense of deprivation in this place like 'a fat black serpent', which was 'alive and breathing, and it couldn't draw breath properly because it was so closely confined between walls and roof; and this was "die lewe" in the prison. The prison itself was a live thing, sweating and suffocating in its own immurement.'[93] Within little more than a decade, political detainees were the ones bearing witness to prison conditions: following the Sharpeville massacre in March 1960, a State of Emergency was declared. In 1961, South Africa left the Commonwealth and was declared a republic. This was a time of great, generalised repression, when under the Sabotage Act it could be considered a crime 'to further or encourage the achievement of any political aim, including the bringing about of any social or economic change in the Republic'.[94]

Over the next four years in particular, there was a marked swelling in the population of political prisoners, drawn from the ranks of a number of armed movements, including Umqonto we Sizwe of the ANC, the PAC and its armed wing Poqo, and the African Resistance Movement where Trotskyists, ex-communists and members of the Liberal Party joined forces. All had decided to engage in a strategy of resistance and sabotage in the wake of the Sharpeville massacre, and were rounded up by the police. Prison writing of the time – almost all of it banned inside the country – included *117 Days* by Ruth First (1965),[95] *The Jail Diary of Albie Sachs* (1966),[96] *Robben Island* (1973)[97] by DM Zwelonke (written in fictional form), *Bandiet* (1974)[98] by Hugh Lewin, and later *Mouroir* (1983)[99] by Breyten

Breytenbach. Writers of different political persuasions each set a vision of despair (and sometimes, as in the case of Zwelonke, the hell of torture) against a sense of political and intellectual purpose. Together, they give credence to Breytenbach's vision of a country 'whose cities were linked by arteries [...] to make travel easier between one prison and another'.[100]

A number of novels were written, and soon banned, engaging with the short-lived revolutionary fervour of the times, including Nadine Gordimer's *The Late Bourgeois World* (1966),[101] Alex La Guma's *The Stone Country* (1967)[102] and *In the Fog of the Season's End* (1972),[103] CJ Driver's *Elegy for a Revolutionary* (1969),[104] Jack Cope's *The Dawn Comes Twice* (1969)[105] and Mary Benson's *At the Still Point* (1971).[106] All these writers had far wider literary ambitions. Cope, for example, apart from being the influential founder, in 1960, of the English and Afrikaans literary magazine *Contrast* and its editor for 20 years, wrote fiction against the backdrop of the rich natural environment of his native Natal, tracing the struggle, and at times complicity, between blacks and whites on both a political and highly personal level. His first novel, *The Fair House* (1955)[107] considers the effects of the 1906 Bambatha Rebellion on later race relations. In the short story 'Flight from Love',[108] the 'witchdoctor' Dismata acts as a catalyst in the destruction of a young white farmer's world; by contrast, in 'The Flight',[109] a white woman, child in arms, escaping from her violent husband, is given desperately needed help by two black men encountered in a forest at night.

Cope and Gordimer were the only two of the writers just mentioned who did not go into exile in the 1960s. If fiction inside the country often remained focused on the human condition under apartheid, works of great diversity were produced by those who left the constraints of this system behind. 'I'm breathing the new air of freedom,' wrote Es'kia Mphahlele from Lagos, Nigeria, on his arrival there in 1957 after finally being granted a passport, 'and now the barrel of gall has no bottom any more.'[110] Mphahlele's *The Wanderers* (1971)[111] recounts the troubles and eventual uneasy exile of a middle-class academic whose son refuses the privileges he now has access to. An earlier work by Peter Abrahams, *A Wreath for Udomo* (1956),[112] relates the way in which an African leader attains power in the fictional country of Panafrica, sacrificing personal integrity in the name of the general good, fighting against tribalism and ultimately being killed by men wearing tribal dress.

In a very different vein, Bessie Head's *A Question of Power* (1974)[113] tells the story of Elizabeth, who, like Head, was the daughter of a white South African woman and her black stable hand. In the midst of a breakdown in a Botswana village, mirrored by the open, fractured structure of the novel, the narrator looks back at the deep alienation of her past, reaching among a cast of half-invented characters for the spiritual power to help her return to her work as a gardener.

Bessie Head went on to write, among other books, *The Collector of Treasures* (1977), a series of tales of everyday village life in Botswana, particularly as seen from a woman's point of view. In the title story, Dikeledi Mokope asks her estranged, abusive husband for money to pay for the education of their son. It is clear that he will give her nothing, yet he sends a note asking her to prepare a meal and a bath for him. She does not immediately know how to respond. 'She had filled her life with treasures of kindness and love she had gathered from others and it was all this that she wanted to protect from defilement by an evil man. Her first panic-stricken thought was to gather up the children and flee the village. But where to go? […] If she wrote back, don't you dare put foot in the yard, I don't want to see you, he would ignore it. Black women didn't have that kind of power.'[114] Instead, she plans a terrible act of revenge, which sharpens the story, underlining both her social condition and her mettle as a person.

Several poets went into exile in the 1960s, among them Dennis Brutus, whose most intensely lyrical poems came from early experience of life inside the country:

> from the shanties creaking iron sheets
> violence like a bug-infested rag is tossed
> and fear is immanent as sound in the wind-swung bell;
> the long day's anger pants from sand and rocks;
> but for this breathing night at least,
> my land, my love, sleep well.[115]

The poetry written by Brutus after he had gone into exile following imprisonment on Robben Island continues to smoulder with anger; behind this emotion, 'the true deep wound that lies/ like the dark bruised pulp at the heart of the fruit'.[116]

One of Brutus's high-school pupils, Arthur Nortje, went overseas in his turn in the 1960s after struggling to get a passport, asking wryly: 'Who loves me so much not to let me go,/ not to let me leave a land of problems?'[117] Nortje's later poetry derives its desperate force from the condition of the outcast: 'The isolation of exile is a gutted/ warehouse at the back of pleasure streets', begins the poem 'Waiting', which ends with the poet having

> [...] vacated the violent arena
> for a northern life of semi-snow

under the Distant Early Warning System:
I suffer the radiation burns of silence.
It is not cosmic immensity or catastrophe
that terrifies me:
it is solitude that mutilates,
the night bulb that reveals ash on my sleeve.[118]

Inside South Africa, with the banning of the ANC and other anti-apartheid parties in the early 1960s, and the arrest, exile or death of their leaders, the role of writers became increasingly politicised; they joined a small minority of people, amongst them artists, lawyers, academics, leaders of student bodies, members of the Anglican and Catholic Churches, as also of the Black Sash, who took a significant public position against state policy. The leeway for legal opposition was slight; correspondingly, the scope of the literary imagination as permitted by the authorities was narrow. This was a time of constant state intervention in all potentially contentious cultural activities. There was increasing political fragmentation as the government pursued a policy of divide and rule, introducing the 'homeland' policy, eliminating 'black spots' of unwanted black communities as part of a general policy of resettlement. The country should put up with black workers by day but remain 'white by night', declared Prime Minister BJ Vorster.

Just a few years earlier, Es'kia Mphahlele had written that 'as long as the white man's politics continue to impose on us a ghetto existence, so long shall the culture and therefore literature of South Africa continue to shrivel up, to sink lower and lower; and for so long shall we in our writing continue to reflect only a minute fraction of life.'[119] Under these conditions, writers voicing what they felt to be the concerns of the people mostly restricted themselves to the mode of testimony and social realism, largely illustrative and often devoid of literary experiment.

At the same time, in the 1960s, certain literary forms became particularly important for their compact brevity, more specifically the short story, the short play and the poem – texts that resonated with a sense of urgency, employing the subterfuge of metaphor, crystallising a message with the effectiveness of a telegram. Coloured poet Adam Small (*Kitaar my Kruis* (Guitar my Cross), 1962), writing in Afrikaans, was among the first to ally the strength of spoken language (in this case, that of the Cape coloured) with the sharp edge of political consciousness, sometimes enriching his words with biblical references, as in the poem 'Groot Krismis Gebied' (Great Krismis Prayer).

> only you can perhaps again
> this Krismas Lord let
> a new Mosas be born for us here
>
> a new Mosas
> a new Mosas –
> o Lord, our Mosas –
> we'll hide him away Lord, we got lotsa hidingplaces
> from the daggers what don' like him –
> to lead us, the whole bunch of us
> lead us to the plain before the vineyards of Canaan.[120]

The late 1960s and early 1970s saw the emergence of several black poets, including Oswald Mtshali, Mongane Wally Serote, Sipho Sepamla and Mafika Gwala, all of them writing in English, as well as Mazisi Kunene, writing from exile in Zulu, which he then translated into English himself. The great attention paid to the first book by any of these poets to appear in South Africa, Mtshali's *Sounds of a Cowhide Drum* (1971), was indicative of the impact of a new kind of voice, directed at both a black and white readership.

It should be mentioned that a number of local publishers came to the fore at this time, including Ad Donker, David Philip and, most radically, Ravan Press, as well as Renoster Books, already in existence for more than a decade, which now sold an unprecedented

16 000 copies of Mtshali's book in the first year. 'I am the drum on your dormant soul,/ cut from the black hide of a sacrificial cow,/ I am the spirit of your ancestors'[121] wrote Mtshali, while at the same time confronting the narrow space of everyday experience with metaphor, as in the poem 'Sunset', here quoted in full:

> The sun spun like
> a tossed coin.
> It whirled on the azure sky,
> it clattered into the horizon,
> it clicked in the slot,
> and neon lights popped
> and blinked 'Time expired',
> as on a parking meter.[122]

Serote, whose lines were often shot through with a similar sense of raw anxiety, notably when speaking of the pressures of Johannesburg, wrote of an overbearing 'dry white season', nonetheless countering the hopelessness of the times with the conclusion that 'seasons come to pass'.[123] Elsewhere, his words are inhabited with a buoyancy absent in local writing for a decade:

> Hell, my mind throbs like a heart beat, there's no
>   peace;

> And my body of wounds – when will they be
>   scars? –
> Yet I can still walk and work and still smile.
> I do not know where I have been,
> But Brother,
> I know I'm coming.
> I do not know where I have been,
> But Brother
> I have a voice like the lightning-thunder over the
> mountains.[124]

Some work of this period did not get passed the censors. *Cry Rage* (1972)[125] by James Matthews and Gladys Thomas was the first collection of poems to be banned in South Africa. Mazisi Kunene's work met a similar fate. Kunene was later known for his ancestral epic poem of 433 pages *Emperor Shaka the Great* (published in English in 1979), which opens with the challenging, celebratory lines:

> Great anthem, by your power break the boundaries
>   of our horizons;
> Fill the wide expanse of the earth with your
>   legendary songs!
> Say then: people have power, people tear the
>   garments of the night;
> By their feet, they scar the grounds with new life.[126]

The black poetry of the 1960s and 1970s can be contrasted with the far more introspective English-speaking white poets of the time, whose uneasy sense of insularity is summed up in the concluding lines of Ruth Miller's poem 'The Floating Island': 'Wrenched from our continent, we blunder/ And lacking weather-sense for guide/ Our green uncharted islands sink in ravelled floods, blind-eyed.'[127] Other white English-speaking poets of this time include Guy Butler (founder of the poetry review *New Coin*) and Sydney Clouts. Like Miller, they often turned to landscape while investigating ways of seeing, means of identity and transcendence. Here is a poem by Clouts, 'Poetry is death cast out':

> Poetry is death cast out
> though it gives one chance to retaliate.
> Death takes it but the poem moves
> a little further beyond death's gate,
>
> And I know the proof of this. Once walking
> amongst bushes and lizard stones I found
> a little further than I had thought
> to go, a stream with a singing sound.[128]

Afrikaans poets of this time include Uys Krige and Ingrid Jonker, remembered above all for her intensely intimate lyrical work, but also for her premonitory poem in response to the turbulence provoked by the Sharpeville massacre, 'Die kind (wat doodgeskiet is deur soldate by Nyanga)' (The child who was shot dead by soldiers at Nyanga):

> The child is not dead
> not at Langa not at Nyanga
> not at Orlando not at Sharpeville
> not at the police station in Philippi
> where he lies with a bullet through his brain
>
> The child is the shadow of the soldiers
> on guard with rifles saracens and batons
> the child is present at all gatherings and law-giving
> the child peers through house windows and into
>   the hearts of mothers
> the child who wanted just to play in the sun at
>   Nyanga is everywhere
> the child grown to a man treks all over Africa
> the child grown to a giant travels through the
>   whole world
>
> Without a pass.[129]

Jonker can be considered a member of the loosely grouped and mainly young Afrikaner writers known as the Sestigers (Writers of the Sixties), among them

Chris Barnard, Breyten Breytenbach, André Brink, Etienne Leroux, Bartho Smit and Abraham de Vries. Inspired by their experience in Europe, and in particular France, as well as by the earlier work of writers such as Jan Rabie and poet Adam Small, they 'consciously introduced the then current vogues of experimentation, existentialism and post-modernism into a literary scene still largely determined by nineteenth century techniques and by the severely localised expression of themes like drought, locusts and poor whites'.[130] The result was a body of work that broke current taboos and conventions, creating severe tension between these writers and the leaders of the highly conservative Afrikaner community who regarded them as traitors: they were failing to play their traditional role as privileged scribes, who might perhaps engage in what NP van Wyk Louw described as 'loyal protest',[131] yet still remained the moral custodians of the tribe.

In Etienne Leroux's *Sewe Dae by die Silbersteins* (*Seven Days at the Silbersteins*, 1962),[132] a tightly constructed novel influenced by Jungian philosophy, Henry van Eeden arrives on a farm to meet his unknown fiancé, Salome. Flawless, angel-faced, unquestioning, over seven days of meetings with different groups of people he undergoes a form of initiation, losing his innocence and becoming aware of the inextricable intertwining of good and evil, and the sharpness of a lonely existence in a dissolute society.

André Brink's first novel, *Kennis van die Aand (Looking on Darkness*, 1973),[133] which tells the story of coloured actor Joseph Malan as he awaits execution for the murder of his white lover, was also the first by an Afrikaner to be banned in South Africa, since it challenged the Immorality Act prohibiting interracial intimacy, and ultimately the moral weight of the entire apartheid system. 'If this is art, then a brothel is a Sunday School,'[134] commented a leading member of the pro-apartheid Dutch Reformed Church.

Extremely prolific, Brink has gone on to create novels that function as mirrors held up to contemporary South African society, as well as reimagining the monolithic state version of its history and the human relations of the past. In *'n Droë Wit Seisoen* (*A Dry White Season*, 1979), which moves at the pace of a detective novel, school history teacher Ben du Toit becomes aware of the daily violence of apartheid as he is personally confronted with the vicious cycle of state violence and in particular the death of his gardener Gordon Ngubene, after being tortured by the police. He also comes to realise the insular nature of white urban life in South Africa. History, a black taxi driver tells him, is not 'made right here where you are and no place else. Why don't you come with me one day, I'll show you what history really looks like. Bare-arsed history, stinking with life. Over at my place, in Sofasonke City'.[135] Shaken out of complacency, Du Toit seeks justice, and pays for this with his own life.

In an earlier work, *An Instant in the Wind* (1976), set in the eighteenth century, a pregnant Afrikaans woman, Elisabeth Louw, encounters runaway slave Adam Mantoor, both of them stranded in the wild interior of the Cape Colony, slowly drawn together, 'round and round, along the endless spiral inward, in to him and her'.[136]

The fact that there has been constant intermixing between people of different colours in South Africa, and that the children of the seventeenth-century Dutch sailors at the Cape were the fruit of union with slave women, was constantly denied under apartheid. Breyten Breytenbach addressed the following comment to a student audience in Cape Town, in 1973: 'We are a bastard people with a bastard language [...] In that part of our blood which comes from Europe was the curse of superiority [...] We made our otherness the norm, the standard – and the ideal. And because our otherness is maintained *at the expense of* our fellow South Africans – and our South Africanhood – we feel threatened. We built walls. Not cities, but city walls. And like all bastards – uncertain of their identity – we began to adhere to the concept of *purity*. That is apartheid. *Apartheid is the law of the bastard.*'[137]

Breytenbach, also a painter, is in many ways the opposite to Brink, intensely personal in much of his poetry, yet questioning any single identity behind 'the mask called Breytenbach'[138] and even when not using surrealist imagery still twisting away from any simple narrative line, at odds with all notions of status quo. Yet he joins Brink in constant return to South African territory, as he did in his first travel account *A Season in Paradise* (1976), or the story of his arrival back in South Africa from Paris in 1975, narrated in *The True Confessions of an Albino Terrorist* (1983),[139] a journey that ended with him receiving a seven-year prison sentence. In one of the poems included in *A Season in Paradise* he speaks of 'my land your land our land/ this land asking for water is given blood/ this land which bears the fire within it'.[140] Here are the beginning and end of another poem from the same book:

> I will die and go to my father
> in Wellington on long legs
> dazzling in the light
> where the rooms are heavy and dark
> where stars sit like seagulls on the rooftop
> and angels dig for worms in the garden
> I will die, pack up a few things
> take the road
> across the Wellington mountains

through the trees and the twilight
and go to my father

[...]

Come with me
bound in my death, to my father
in Wellington where the angels
use worms to fish fat stars from heaven;
let us die and decompose and be merry:
my father has a large boarding house.[141]

By the early 1970s there was a rise in the political temperature in South Africa. Dockworkers in Durban, who had already gone on strike in 1969, did so again in 1972, this time joined by others in Cape Town. More than 300 strikes took place in the country in 1973 and 1974, many of them brutally repressed. In 1975, Frelimo won independence for Mozambique after a protracted guerrilla war with Portuguese and South African forces; news of this victory spread through the townships on transistor radios. The Black Consciousness movement gathered momentum, inspired partly by the Black Power movement in the United States, backed by black student and radical church organisations, calling for a sense of black identity, community development and power.

For political reasons, and as a premonitory act before the Soweto Uprising of 1976, the poet Adam Small, like other writers such as Achmat Dangor, renounced the idea of writing in Afrikaans, preferring the use of English in the 50 quatrains of his book *Black Bronze Beautiful* (1975) to affirm the sensual power but also ancestral subordination of his people:

> Pluck at my pomegranate breasts and throw each
>   purple pip
> Back of your open throat; don't fear the full feast
> Of this seed so rich: for in this joy of flesh
> Is blended pain also – the slave-chain and the
>   whip[142]

The potent juxtaposition of pleasure and pain, light and darkness, is present with a particular racial undertone in several works by coloured writers. The question of coloured identity is rarely far away. Arthur Nortje, referring in one poem to a white 'Strongman' who 'was blond & I black', says 'I had seen and spoken to the light/ though at any time he could call the darkness back'.[143] The unnamed coloured man in Richard Rive's story 'Make like slaves' drives with a white woman to a play rehearsal she is running with black schoolchildren from Nyanga township, at a community centre outside Cape Town. 'It raised complications to drive around a coloured male. So-called coloured male. She mentally played with the words. Capital C or small c? Coloured gentleman. How did they say again at drama school? Gentleman of colour.'[144] The theme of her play is the American slavery story, and the man bears speechless witness as she asks five young actors to 'start with the third act. I want you to make like slaves.'[145]

Other writing is torn with the destruction of residential areas, too close to the white city as far as the authorities were concerned. In Achmat Dangor's novella 'Waiting for Leila', the narrator Samad associates expropriation with the loss of the woman he loves: 'Jackhammers picking like crows at his guts. All around him they were breaking down his city, brick by brick, stone for stone. District Six – Rock Of My History! Leila! Where the hell are you?'[146] In *The Visitation*, a novel by Indian writer Ahmed Essop, the businessman Mr Emir Sufi, passively sunk in his own opulence and pawn to the ruthless gangster Gool, is finally persuaded that he should sell his Fordsburg properties adjoining Johannesburg and invest rather in 'Elysia' to which Indians will be removed. This he does though he knows that 'the Orient Front and the People's Movement had condemned Elysia as a racial ghetto'.[147]

Denis Hirson

※

In the 1960s and 1970s the theatre became a particularly potent form of expression in South Africa. In 1959, the 'all-African jazz opera' *King Kong* had been written by Harry Bloom, with lyrics by Pat Williams and a musical score by Todd Matshikiza (who also wrote music reviews for *Drum* magazine). This play, which had considerable local and international success and led to the 'discovery' of leading actress Miriam Makeba, celebrated township life while telling the story of the rise and fall of local boxing hero Ezekiel Dhlamini. *King Kong* was itself produced in the face of apartheid's daily obstacles. When it had been on for a week in Johannesburg, a leading actor and a friend of his were arrested without a pass and forced to work for the day in a policeman's garden, only to be told at the end of the day, 'You've been good boys and worked well. You can go now.' The actor only just managed to arrive back in time for that night's performance.[148]

Not long after *King Kong's* box office-breaking run, black playwright Gibson Kente began writing 'township musicals' of his own, often situated in a township shebeen, speaking to township audiences of local hardship, providing comic relief as well as sequences of African jazz and gospel. Later plays, still filled with humour, wordplay and township slang, were pointedly political, expressing the severe limits placed by the apartheid system on the lives of the protagonists. *How Long* (1973) recounts the story of a dustman determined to provide his son, Africa, with the funds to stay in school. Zwelthsa, the Xhosa protagonist of *I Believe* (1974), falls in love with a woman from a different tribe. Here is an extract from *Too Late* (1975),[149] in which the orphan Saduva comes to Soweto to live with his shebeen-queen aunt, but struggles to get a pass in order to work. Originally published in the literary review *S'ketsh'*,[150] the script below was altered after the banning of the review:

> *Police sirens – panic, panic, panic. Men immediately frisk their pockets, making sure they have their pass books.*
> *Enter* **Madinto, Saduva** *and* **Totozi** *running, carrying liquor. Sirens are synchronised with orchestra. Movement on stage is in dance form, rhythmic. Men search their pockets in rhythm.*
> **Mfundisi** [*searching for his pass in rhythm too*]: Where is it?
> **Pelepele**: I forgot it.
> **Sguqa**: I lost it.
> **Diza**: I haven't got it.
> **Saduva** [*frightened*]: I won't get it.

Offside: I never had it.
Doctor: I don't want it.
Music stops.[151]

At the same time as Kente was producing his plays, two other men came to the fore who were to change the face of South African theatre: Barney Simon and Athol Fugard. Simon was editor (1964–1971) of the influential literary journal *The Classic*[152] and author of the short-story collection *Jo'burg, Sis* (1974).[153] But he worked above all as a theatre director, staging multiracial performances wherever he could, in warehouses, townships, and such non-segregated venues as the Bantu Men's Social Centre in Johannesburg. In 1976, with Mannie Manim and others, he co-founded Johannesburg's central theatre venue, The Market Theatre. Simon's general aim was, through plays workshopped with the actors themselves, to reflect the many faces of South African culture. Noting that blacks were treated as no more than shadows by whites, he affirmed that 'What I try to do in my work always is to give identity to the shadows.'[154] Like Athol Fugard, he encouraged actors to use authentic South African language, stripping away the false British accent that had previously dominated the stage. Above all, both of them set out to unflinchingly bear witness to the society around them.

Fugard, working with Samuel Becket's sense of spareness and absurdity, influenced also by Jerzy Grotowski's 'poor theatre' and the idea of quintessential human presence on the stage, pursued two avenues in his early plays. Firstly, he revealed the reality of township life to central city audiences, showing blacks under constant threat of white laws and black gangsters in *No-Good Friday* (1958); telling the story of a woman who had been a mineworkers' whore in *Nongogo* (1959).[155] In *The Blood Knot* (1961),[156] two half-brothers – one of them coloured and the other black – share a shack, almost destroying each other as they play out a racist game, but ultimately reconciled thanks to their 'blood knot'. Later, *Boesman and Lena* (1969)[157] follows a coloured couple whose squatter house has once again been destroyed by white bulldozers, out across a wasteland of mud, violent bickering and miraculous survival. On the other hand, in a play such as the partly autobiographical *Hello and Goodbye* (1965),[158] Fugard develops the theme of dispossession, this time among poor whites: a jobless young man walks around a house on his dead father's crutches, and is visited by his prostitute sister who has come to claim what she believes is left of their father's money.

In 1962, noting that most theatre performances were being performed before segregated audiences, Fugard wrote a letter that precipitated the boycott of

South African theatre by most English-speaking overseas playwrights.[159] Culture became an even more intensely political arena, with the regime clamping down on events of all kinds. Soon, theatre casts and audiences were entirely segregated by law.

In the early 1970s, Fugard continued an earlier collaboration with the black Serpent Players (a group he had founded with residents of New Brighton township, outside Port Elizabeth). He worked with actors John Kani and Winston Ntshona to create two plays giving voice to black resilience: *Sizwe Banzi is Dead* (1972), concerning a man who takes on a dead man's identity in order to use his pass and survive in the city, and *The Island* (1972), about two prisoners on Robben Island who, among other things, engage in a production of Sophocles's *Antigone*.

> **John.** Antigone, you have pleaded guilty. Is there anything you wish to say in mitigation? This is your last chance to speak. Speak.
> **Winston.** Who made the law forbidding the burial of my brother?
> **John.** The State.
> **Winston.** Who is the State?
> **John.** As King I am its manifest symbol.
> **Winston.** So you made the law.
> **John.** Yes, for the State.

Winston. Are you God?
John. Watch your words, little girl!
Winston. You said it was my turn to speak.
John. But not to ridicule.
Winston. I've got no time to waste on that. Your sentence on my life hangs waiting on your lips.
John. Then speak on.[160]

Radical collaborative, multiracial theatre was produced by Robert McLaren and his group Workshop '71 in Johannesburg, aiming to use theatre as 'a means of mass organisation, mobilisation and conscientisation',[161] ultimately working only with black actors as Black Consciousness ideology became increasingly significant. The group's first play, *Crossroads* (1971), was based on the mediaeval morality play *Everyman*. In 1972, in Cape Town's The Space theatre, a second influential multiracial theatre company was founded by Athol Fugard, actors John Kani and Yvonne Bryceland and Paul Slabolepszy (later to become one of the country's most prolific playwrights). Here, the opening event was Fugard's *Statements After an Arrest under the Immorality Act* (1972).[162]

When Soweto and other townships exploded in 1976, with schoolchildren going out into the streets rather than accepting Afrikaans as a medium of instruction, only to be violently repressed, Black

Consciousness playwrights such as Maishe Maponya (*Peace and Forgive* (1977) and *The Hungry Earth* (1981))[163] caught the mood of revolt. The song 'Wake up mother Afrika [...] before the white man rapes you' sets the tone for the latter.[164] In his militant play *Egoli* (1979),[165] Matsemela Manaka's characters speak cuttingly of the living conditions of migrant mineworkers. Underlining the political vacuum of the times, though with considerable humour, Barney Simon, Percy Mtwa and Mbongeni Ngema (the latter two having previously worked with Gibson Kente) staged their play *Woza Albert!* (Arise, Albert [Luthuli]! 1980)[166] with reference to the one-time president of the ANC and Nobel Peace Prize winner. Here, Christ arrives in Soweto by air from Johannesburg, people's reactions to him revealing the ridiculous side of apartheid. In the final scene, Christ is called upon to awaken all the heroes of the liberation struggle.

In the 1980s, in Natal, a play such as the *Dunlop Play* (1983), about worker history, was developed by a group of workers, including Alfred Temba Qabula and Nise Malange. This, says writer and trade-unionist Ari Sitas, actively present at the time, was part of the cultural action engaged in under difficult circumstances to break down 'barriers between different unions and groups of workers – and also between workers and their families; and between the factory and the community.'[167]

From the refracted angle of exile, on the other hand, events within the country took on a different aspect. Zakes Mda, in *We Shall Sing for the Fatherland* (1977)[168] – the first of several plays on the same theme–was already lamenting that a new government, craving power and as corrupt as the old one, would betray the ideals of resistance. Mda's theme was new in the South African context, his story strengthened by drawing on the tradition of Xhosa storytelling known as *intsomi*, 'an enactment, an event, a ritual, a performance […]'.[169]

When it came to shorter literary forms, in South Africa itself many voices found an outlet as of 1977 in the magazine *Staffrider*, a publishing response to the student revolt of 1976, as well as to the huge revival of poetry, forged into a political weapon through the Black Consciousness cultural movement. *Staffrider*'s name itself reveals the mood of the times, referring to young black men who risked death by riding on top of and outside 'the fast and dangerous trains of our late seventies'.[170] The editors of the magazine at one time or another included Mike Kirkwood of Ravan Press, Chris van Wyk, Andries Oliphant, Ivan Vladislavic, Frank Meintjies and Mi S'Dumo Hlatshwayo. Included in its pages, apart from photographs and drawings, were short stories, poems and essays by a vast array of writers, many but not all of them politically dissenting writers of the time. They included Mothobe Mutloatse, Ahmed Essop, Achmat Dangor, Njabulo S Ndebele, Kelwyn Sole, Douglas Livingstone, Richard Rive, Andries Oliphant, Chris van Wyk, Mafika Gwala, Rose Zwi, Farouk Asvat, Mongane Wally Serote and Hugh Lewin. Several of them would go on to or had already published works looking hard at life under apartheid, such as Miriam Tlali's autobiographical novel *Muriel at Metropolitan* (1975),[171] Mtutuzeli Matshoba's collection of short stories *Call me not a Man* (1979)[172] and Andries Oliphant's collection of poems *At the End of the Day* (1988) in which he asks 'Oh, land shaped like a heart/ why are you always letting blood?'[173] Kelwyn Sole, in his first book of poems, *The Blood of our Silence* (1988) speaks of

[...] a history
made malignant in the heart,
where I seek you
seeking a lost harmony of tongues.[174]

Chris van Wyk's poems, collected in *It's Time to Go Home* (1979), include one written in 1976 that looks back at the patently untrue police claims concerning prison deaths a few years earlier, and turns them into bitter laughter:

> He fell from the ninth floor
> He hanged himself
> He slipped on a piece of soap while washing
> He hanged himself
> He slipped on a piece of soap while washing
> He fell from the ninth floor
> He hanged himself while washing
> He slipped from the ninth floor
> He hung from the ninth floor
> He slipped on the ninth floor while washing
> He fell from a piece of soap while slipping
> He hung from the ninth floor
> He washed from the ninth floor while slipping
> He hung from a piece of soap while washing[175]

Not all the writing published in *Staffrider* referred directly to the political situation. A story such as Bheki Maseko's 'Mamlambo' (1982)[176] brings an ancestral yet vitally present world of tribal magic into the white residential suburbs of Johannesburg. It recounts the efforts of Sophie Zikode to maintain a relationship with her new Malawian lover Jonas. A consultation with a local street sweeper who is also a 'traditional doctor' ultimately results in her waking up to find under her pillow the snake of good and ill fortune Mamlambo.

She must at all costs get rid of this snake if she is to keep Jonas. Maseko was one of a number of storytellers to turn to the written page, recounting a tale from which whites are virtually absent, though the context is a predominantly white city.

Staffrider found a place for voices that had never previously been heard; some were never to be heard of again. Here for example is 'Wooden Spoon', one of two poems by K Zwide, of whom nothing else is known, recording something of the implosive despair felt in the wake of 1976 and resonant with failed ancestral revolt:

> I carved a spoon from a rose-root
> and, though thornless, its shape was strange,
> conforming with the twisted nature
> of the rose's journey into the earth.
>
> Grandfather carved a straight spear
> of a fine yellow wood;
> melted ironstone with oxfat
> and beat the blade on a rock,
> and, blessing it with leaves and milk,
> he whirled it into the air.
> In response to gravity
> it pierced his heart.
>
> Now I eat with a crooked spoon

which I have dug from my master's garden
and it pierces my heart.[177]

Another writer who contributed to *Staffrider* was the already well-established novelist, poet and literary critic Lionel Abrahams, founder of the magazine *The Purple Renoster* in 1956 and Renoster Press in 1957, someone who was for decades a highly influential mentor to many writers. Elsewhere, Abrahams set down the malaise of white suburban existence in lines such as

We can afford to say we know
the blacks are really given hell,
Big Boss is harsh and stupid and must go:
we say it – and it helps like one Aspro.
We still feel jumpy, mixed up, not quite well.[178]

In contrast, the poet Wopko Jensma, writing in both Afrikaans and English, adding in township slang, sought to break out of the strictures of a white existence, inventing a local raw blues-like voice. Probably because of the way he himself had crossed racial barriers, Jensma was able like no one before him to simultaneously take into account, in the fractured music of his language, both white and black experience. In one poem, 'Spanner in the What? Works', Jensma speaks of his own birth and death as if they had occurred in several places, each of them specific to a different racial group under apartheid. The 'I' in this poem is thus multiple, and all the more vulnerable since it bears the deeply cracked imprint of the society as a whole:

> i hope to live to the age of sixty
> i hope to leave some evidence
> that i inhabited this world
> that i sensed my situation
> that i created something
> out of my situation
> out of my life
> that i lived
> as human
> alive
> i[179]

By the late 1970s and early 1980s, with the Soweto revolt quashed, the Black Consciousness leader Steve Biko tortured and killed in prison, and censors still working assiduously (under apartheid, an estimated 18 000 books were banned),[180] a few established South African writers occupied a substantial place in the world of South African letters, despite themselves being affected by censorship and other state restrictions. These included playwright Athol Fugard (*A Lesson from Aloes*, 1978, *Master Harold ... and the Boys*, 1982),[181] novelist André Brink (*A Chain of Voices*, 1981, *Mapmakers: Writing in a State of Siege*, 1983),[182] poet and novelist Mongane Wally Serote to whom I will return, and two other writers, Nadine Gordimer and JM Coetzee.

With some notable exceptions, Gordimer's short-story collections have tended to focus above all on the intimacy of human relations, particularly in South Africa. Her essays on writing and the place of the writer in society (*The Essential Gesture*, 1988)[183] have often spoken out against both oppression and complacency. Her novels, less didactic and highly intricate, have consistently charted the evolution of South African society, sharing a vision of what critic Stephen Clingman terms 'history from the inside'.[184] Gordimer hopes not only to bear witness, but through works of the imagination to engage dialectically with the historical process itself.

Burger's Daughter (1979)[185] charts the life of Rosa Burger, daughter of Lionel Burger, an Afrikaner political prisoner who dies in jail as did his model, Bram Fischer, the advocate and communist leader descended from a major statesman of the Orange Free State republic. The novel follows Rosa Burger's quest for love, but also shows her response to the Black Consciousness movement and the 1976 Soweto revolt. *July's People* (1981)[186] imagines a country where cities have become battlegrounds, and whites are fleeing for their lives. Above all, it explores the inversion of power relations as the family of Bam and Maureen Smales, enlightened and liberal whites, is offered refuge in a village by their black servant July.

Perhaps the most accomplished and symbolically most powerful of Gordimer's novels during this period was *The Conservationist* (1974), written at a time when white farmers faced uncertainty in both Zimbabwe and Mozambique, where colonial regimes were challenged by revolutionary movements. The novel focuses on the moment when businessman Mehring is confronted with the body of a black worker, murdered and buried on his farmland, and uncovered during a storm. Ultimately unable to deal with this event, he leaves the farm, 'for one of those countries white people go to, the whole world is theirs'.[187] The black workers bury the body, 'put him to rest, at last; he had come back. He took possession of this earth, theirs; one of them.'[188] The substantial literary absence of blacks from the *plaasroman* and Schreiner's *The Story of an African Farm* is reversed with this return, while the reader might be reminded of the ANC slogan 'Afrika! Mayibuye!' (Africa! May it come back!).[189]

Nadine Gordimer won the Nobel Prize for Literature in 1991, as did JM Coetzee in 2003. Though in general Coetzee was against the subjection of fiction to history, he does make reference to the violent colonial history of his own forebears (*Dusklands*, 1974).[190] He too has in several works written of black-white relations on a farm, for example in *In The Heart of the Country* (1977).[191] He too has written a novel imagining a post civil-war South Africa, *Life & Times of Michael K* (1983).[192] Like Fugard, he is of both English-speaking and Afrikaner descent, which gives their work a particular form of double-rootedness in the South African context.

One central way in which certain novels by Coetzee can be distinguished from those by many of his contemporaries concerns the different devices he has employed to shift away from direct, frontal reference to the realities of South Africa. The narrator of *In the Heart of the Country* is unreliable, a quality that opens out all the possible, extreme, dreamed relationships of power and intimacy between a farmer, his daughter, their black worker and his wife. The sense of simultaneous multiple realities is encoded in the book's structure: it is written in numbered paragraphs, in which the same events re-occur, seen from different angles.

In *Waiting for the Barbarians* (1980),[193] the story of a

magistrate who seeks peace between his own military regime and a neighbouring 'barbarian' people, the landscape is not recognisably South African, nor is the epoch clearly defined. The focus is on the nature of relations between Colonel Joll of the Third Bureau of the Civil Guard and the Magistrate, between the Magistrate and a 'barbarian' woman, in the context of a historically undefined colonial empire. Despite potential references to the doings of the secret police in South Africa, 'this could be the Roman Empire, the Gestapo, the Lubyanka prison, or Abu Ghraib; unfortunately, the world keeps inventing new contexts for this novel'.[194]

The distancing, widening effect of Coetzee's work, the atmosphere of parable, is heightened by the constant resonance with other literary works. Stylistically, the spare, precise prose has affinities with Beckett. *Waiting for the Barbarians* is contiguous with Kafka's 'In the Penal Colony'. The narrator of *Foe* (1986),[195] Susan Barton, has been shipwrecked with a white man named Cruso, and returns to seventeenth-century London with a black, tongueless companion, Friday. Dante and Virgil are not far from the hell of the townships described in *Age of Iron* (1990). A child leaves a township strewn with houses on fire, wet ash and burning rubber: 'With entire self-assurance, greeting us all with a smile, he got into the car and began to give directions. Ten years old at most. A child of the times, at home in this landscape of violence. When I think back to my own childhood I remember only long sun-struck afternoons, the smell of dust under avenues of eucalyptus, the quiet rustle of water in roadside furrows, the lulling of doves. A childhood of sleep, prelude to what was meant to be a life without trouble and a smooth passage to Nirvana. Will we at least be allowed our Nirvana, we children of that bygone age? I doubt it. If justice reigns at all, we will find ourselves barred at the first threshold of the underworld. White as grubs in our swaddling bands, we will be dispatched to join those infant souls whose eternal whining Aeneas mistook for weeping.'[196]

Another novelist who, like Coetzee and Gordimer, wrote of a post-civil war South Africa, focusing on the defeated and demoralised whites rather than black or coloured survivors, was Karel Schoeman, in *Na die Geliefde Land* (*Promised Land*, 1972).[197] *Afskeid en Vertrek* (*Take Leave and Go*, 1990)[198] speaks of an Afrikaner faced with chaos in South Africa in the 1970s, who has the courage to stay when his companion leaves. Between these two books, Schoeman published, among others, *'n Ander Land* (*Another Country*, 1984),[199] set in the nineteenth century, during which a Dutchman convalescing from tuberculosis travels from Europe to Bloemfontein seeking not only health but total detachment in the sparse, unsparing landscape.

Going back still further in time, in *Die kremetartekspedisie* (The Expedition to the Baobab Tree, 1981), poet and novelist Wilma Stockenström traces the journey of a seventeenth-century slave woman away from the Cape, where those of her kind were all 'frightened mice in the middle of a great roaring, [...] our children taken away from us and sold while still infants, while our bodies still hungered for them, our past a past of pitiless treatment or the sarcasm of gifts'.[200] She survives a disastrous expedition led by her last master and protector into the interior of the country, now entirely lucid about her past yet hopelessly isolated as she takes refuge like a bat with folded wings in the darkness of a baobab tree.

Both Schoeman and Stockenström reached deeply into the resources of a literary imagination at a time when the spectacle of violence in the society around them was on a scale beyond belief. In a 1984 essay, Njabulo S Ndebele discusses the way in which this situation led to what he terms 'spectacular demonstration' in black South African writing, filled with predictable caricature, devoid of detailed observation, surprise or analysis: 'Thinking is secondary to seeing. Subtlety is secondary to obviousness. What is left and what is deeply etched in our minds is the spectacular contest between the powerless and the powerful. Most of the time the contest ends in horror and tragedy for the powerless. Sometimes there are victories, but they are always proportionately secondary to the massively demonstrated horror that has gone before.'[201]

Mongane Serote's novel *To Every Birth its Blood* (1981) is an interesting test of this statement. Split in two, its first half – probably set before 1976 – is filled with detailed description of the state of mind and body of narrator Tsi Mohope, dark with stories of arrest and the constant threat of prison, referring constantly to the humiliation of blacks, notably the narrator's own father: 'Every time I look at you I see a terrible, a brutal defeat.'[202] Desire, and the desire for music, appear as the only antidotes to this condition: 'That moment, as she went about the house opening the windows, taking off her shoes, unbuttoning her blouse, looking calm and more friendly, I wanted to weep. I did not know how I was going to tell her, "Baby, most things about this earth make you want to run, want to make you weary, want you to faint." So I sat back on the chair. I said, "Honey, why don't you play Nina Simone?"'[203] Yet virility itself is held in check, the narrator speaking of 'my helplessness, my despair, my anger; my limp muscle, which lay looped as if it were ashamed to have ever erected'.[204]

In the second half of the book there is constant

reference to 'the power years' immediately following June 1976. There is a war on, individuals have lost all sense of intimacy and are preoccupied only with the guerrilla tactics of 'the Movement', but are either killed or forced into exile as their strategies prove to be unsuccessful. And still the novel, which ends with a woman giving birth, affirms that resistance is engrained among the oppressed: 'The Movement is old. It is as old as the grave of the first San or Khoikhoi who was killed by a bullet that came from a ship which had anchored at Cape Town to establish a stop station. The Movement is as young as the idea of throwing stones, of hurling one's life at the young men who believe in God and shoot with guns. The Movement is the eyes which see how poverty is akin to a skeleton. So white. So dry.' [205]

Ndebele answered his own challenge with his book of short stories *Fools and Other Stories* (1984), foregoing the use of fiction as a rallying cry, choosing in the place of black powerlessness to explore the resilience of everyday life in the townships, particularly as seen through the eyes of a child. In 'The Prophetess', a prophetess blesses water that a boy will take home to his ailing mother, intoning: 'If the reeds in winter/ can dry up and seem dead/ and then rise/ in the spring,/ we too will survive the fire that is coming.'[206] Whatever he may think of this potentially political message, the boy later hears the powers of the prophetess being questioned on a bus, his initiatory days filled with far more questions than certainties. 'It is the fairy tale in me,/ the story book/ that is the pure tale of my being,'[207] says Ndebele in a poem that pleads against cultural caricature, and his stories are filled with the rich contradictions of human perception. The prophetess, far from the otherworldly character the township-dwellers believe her to be, impresses on the boy the need to master words and take responsibility for his own acts, rather than bending his awe to her own purposes. 'My son, she tells him, we are made of all that is in the world. Go. Go and heal your mother.'[208]

Another book to follow a similar, complex approach is Zoë Wicomb's, *You Can't Get Lost in Cape Town* (1987), a collection of short stories about a coloured girl growing up in Cape Town, leaving and then returning. The narrative moves constantly between the fine, wry examination of relationships, and the description of moments reaching a symbolic pitch. In 'A Trip to the Gifberge' a daughter returns from London to Cape Town to resume a traumatic relationship with her mother, and at one point pours her some tea. 'I do not anticipate the hand thrust out to take the drink so that I come too close and the liquid lurches into the saucer. The dry red earth laps up the offering of spilled infusion which turns into a patch of fresh blood.'²⁰⁹ In the same story, the protea, perceived by the daughter as the national flower of the whites and rejected as such, becomes both a symbol of reconciliation with her mother and an affirmation of deeply shared identity, rooted in the longer histories of the land itself. 'You who're so clever ought to know that proteas belong in the veld,' says the mother. 'Only fools and cowards would hand them over to the Boers […] We know who lived in these mountains when the Europeans were still shivering in their own country. What they think of the veld and its flowers is of no interest to me.'²¹⁰

These works by Ndebele and Wicomb (like Serote's novel) were written outside South Africa, their vision and emotion sharpened with distance, and, in Serote's case, with militant political engagement. Meanwhile, inside the country there was turmoil. The mid-1980s were ablaze with strikes, consumer boycotts and political funerals violently disrupted by police and soldiers, leading to further funerals. Story-teller, actress and writer Gcina Mhlophe, in her 1986 poem 'The Dancer', speaks of her mother being a beautiful wedding dancer while she herself, amongst those 'running fast with the coffin/ of a would-be bride or a would-be groom', has become a funeral dancer.²¹¹

The government's 1984 establishment of a tricameral parliament, offering the Indian and coloured communities a puppet role while there would be no representation at all for blacks, was largely shunned by all but the majority of the whites themselves. From outside the country, ANC president Oliver Tambo stated that Indians accepting this new dispensation would be 'selling [their] birthright for a mess of pottage'.[212] Inside the country the United Democratic Front (UDF) was formed, bringing together largely ANC-linked grassroots organisations and trade unions to oppose the 1984 national elections. Unrest was so great that in 1985 a partial State of Emergency was declared, followed by a full State of Emergency one year later.

Creative responses in language to the urgent pressures of the time were not confined to the written page. In one essay,[213] Jeremy Cronin sets side by side various forms of what he terms 'insurgent poetry', including poems spoken by those about to be hanged, word-fragments on prison walls or left behind under pillows by children fleeing the townships, chants of toyi-toyi protesters, as well as poems of one sort or another performed in response to popular demand during meetings and conferences, some of them 'lovingly transcribed' by police informers. Cronin himself transcribes one of these poems:

Cuppa-ta-lismmmma, cuppa-ta-lismma,

> A spectre is a hauntinnnga you
> This accordinnnga the gospel
> Of Marx and Engels
> Cuppa-ta-lissssmmma!

As a political prisoner, Cronin himself sought

> To voice without swallowing
> Syllables born in tin shacks, or catch
> The 5.15 ikwata bust fife
> Chwannisberg train, to reach
> The low chant of the mine gang's
> Mineral glow of our people's unbreakable resolve.
>
> To learn how to speak
> With the voices of this land.[214]

Meanwhile, poets such as Mzwake Mbuli, Aubrey Mokoena, Keith Gottschalk and Peter Horn read before thousands at mass rallies, joined (notably in the province of Natal) by others who were themselves workers. These included Alfred Temba Qabula, Nise Malange and Mi S'Dumo Hlatshwayo, who said of himself: 'I wanted to be a poet, control words, many words, that I may woo our multicultured South Africa into a single society [...] After 34 years of hunger, suffering, struggles, learning and hope, I am only a driver for a rubber company.'²¹⁵ Here is the end section of Hlatshwayo's poem, 'The Black Mamba Rises', whose full power can only be gauged if one imagines the popular response, including the slogan-chanting and ululation in the course of an oral performance:

> Tell them – the borrowed
> Must be given back,
> Tell them – the chained
> Must be chained no more,
> Tell them – these are the
> Dictates of the black mamba,
> The mamba that knows no
> Colour,
> Tell them – these are the
> Workers' demands,
> By virtue of their birthright
> Dunlop workers I'm taking
> My hat off,
> I'm bowing to you with
> Respect.²¹⁶

By 1987, the year in which South African forces were defeated in Angola with the help of Cuban soldiers, President PW Botha had begun negotiating Nelson

Mandela's release from prison. In 1989 – the same year in which the USSR collapsed, along with the Berlin Wall – FW de Klerk took over from Botha, overseeing Mandela's release one week after the legalisation of the ANC, the PAC and the Communist Party. Teams led by De Klerk and Mandela sat at the negotiating table, acts of violence were perpetrated from one end of the political spectrum to the other, the extreme right threatened civil war, while waves of fear, doubt and excitement broke against each other throughout the country. Exiles returned to meet those who had never left and for some of whom 'there was no worse exile than home'.[217]

During the late 1980s and early 1990s, several works of autobiography, or journalism with an autobiographical slant, subjected the country to fresh scrutiny. Mark Mathabane's *Kaffir Boy* (1986)[218] gives a stark anatomy of daily life among the desperately poor under apartheid, detailing the miracle of survival in the face of an incessant winding procession of hostile characters, including administrators, policemen and gangs whose violence is echoed by that of the author's own relentlessly unsympathetic father. In *African Women* (1994),[219] Mathabane extends his picture to include four generations of women in his family, whose sense of resilience is tested not only by the outside world but by the men in their lives. Sindiwe Magona's memoir *To My*

Children's Children (1991) reveals apartheid South Africa through the eyes of a woman who was once a teacher, constrained to take on a series of menial jobs. As a maid, she notes that one employer 'often made me feel I was stronger than she was. Not physically. She had this air of fearfulness that was incomprehensible to the likes of me. Weren't all whites omnipotent?'[220]

A sense of fear also runs down the spine of Rian Malan's *My Traitor's Heart* (1990), in which he investigates, through a series of case studies, the deep-rooted forces of ancestry 'and the ancient mysteries of race, the strange forces that put me to bed with a gun and a knife and eventually sent me scurrying out of my country like a coward'.[221] Much of Malan's book takes place in Natal, which is also the setting for Ernst Havemann's short story collection *Bloodsong* (1987). In the title story, which perhaps takes place in the 1930s, a white boy allows Zulus to take the 'Path of the Ancients' so as to cross his father's farm for a ceremonial gathering. That same night he is terrified to find them dancing in battle with shields and sticks, forming an impi and chanting a battle cry in the cornfields close to the farmhouse. Then, switching from aggression to supplication, they respectfully ask for water, and, just that once, tell him, 'You are one of us'.[222]

Christopher Hope's journalistic *White Boy Running* (1988) covers the last whites-only elections of 1987, and renders a picture of absurdity, the country 'a deeply inventive asylum where the inmates long ago took over the running of the institution, dressed up in white coats, and have been giving orders ever since'.[223] Hope, equally a poet (one-time editor of the Natal literary magazine *Bolt*, founded by Ian Glenn) and established novelist, looks back at life in a Johannesburg suburb through a prism of comic surrealism in *The Love Songs of Nathan J Swirsky* (1993).[224] A surrealist view of politics is also a central ingredient of Mike Nicol's novels, such as *The Powers That Be* (1989),[225] in which an entire Cape fishing village is subjugated to the iron laws of Captain Nunes. Ivan Vladislavic's short story collection *Missing Persons* (1989) swirls with displaced objects and events from the apartheid era, including a monument, the body of Dr HF Verwoerd, the diary of his assassin, but also a hand that suddenly bursts into flame and comes to rest on a cashier's thigh, and a mundane pile of building bricks that will be used to build a wall, meanwhile leading the narrator to realise that his own house is collapsing: 'The bricks began to peel away from the walls in squadrons and they flew down to my neighbour's house and assembled themselves into barbecues and watchtowers and gazebos and rondawels and bomb shelters. When all the walls had unravelled completely I was left floating on the raft of the floor.'[226]

Vladislavic's first novel, *The Folly* (1993), similarly centres on the tenuousness of building construction. On the neglected plot of land he has inherited the protagonist Nieuwenhuizen seems to be using little more than his own imagination to build a house, rather than the string, nails and rubbish at his disposal, while the realities of South Africa hover menacingly in the distance like a TV show being watched by the neighbours: 'The box brought nothing but unrest and disorder, faction fights and massacres, even bloodbaths, high pressure systems and cold fronts, situation comedies and real life dramas [...] Each new atrocity struck Mrs like a blow.'[227]

As early as 1981, Nadine Gordimer had quoted Gramsci as an epigraph to *July's People*: 'The old is dying and the new cannot be born; in this interregnum there arises a great diversity of morbid symptoms.'[228] Perhaps the novel that encapsulates this thought more tellingly than any other is Mark Behr's *Die Reuk van Appels* (*The Smell of Apples*, 1993).[229] Here currents of memory interweave as the narrator Marnus Erasmus relates his time as a lieutenant in the 1987 war against Angola, but also his childhood love for the same father who as an army officer himself engages in military deals with a member of the Chilean junta, as well as sodomising Marnus's best friend Frikkie.

Through all the uncertainty the country waited, like

the woman in Gordimer's short story 'Amnesty' (from her collection *Jump and Other Stories*, 1991) whose husband had returned from Robben Island but was too busy with political organisation to relate to her or their young daughter at all, hardly visiting the house that they shared, so that she was left 'Waiting for him to come back. Waiting. I'm waiting to come back home'.[230]

In the theatre, several productions in the mid-1980s brought to the stage events of the recent past. Mbongeni Ngema's play *Sarafina!* (1986)[231] – a musical celebrating the Soweto children's revolt of a decade earlier – later became a Broadway hit. Malcolm Purkey, theatre director of the Junction Avenue Theatre Company, which had been founded in 1976, with 'an obsession to reclaim and popularise the hidden history of struggle in our country', produced *Sophiatown* (1986),[232] focusing on the period when black residents were removed from this area. At another level, *Poppie Nongena* (1984), adapted for the stage by Sandra Kotze from the novel *Die Swerfjare van Poppie Nongena* (*The Long Journey of Poppie Nongena*), by Elsa Joubert,[233] tells of 10 years of resistance against the pass laws by a black woman who wants to keep her family together and is ultimately forcibly removed from Cape Town to a township hundreds of miles away in East London.

Other plays from the mid-1980s responded directly to the political turmoil of the times. *Born in the RSA* (1985),[234] directed by Barney Simon, is about six characters ensnared in a web of relations with a white student turned police informer. *Bopha* (Arrest, 1986),[235] by Percy Mtwa, centres on confrontation between a black policeman and his son, a leader of the 1976 Soweto revolt; in the same year *Wathint' abafazi, wathint' imbokodo* ('You Strike the Woman, You Strike the Rock', a reference to a slogan used during the womens' protest march on the Union Buildings in 1956),[236] directed by Phyllis Klotz, recounts the plight of three women hawkers abandoned not only by white society but also by their own menfolk. Mbongeni Ngema's slightly earlier *Asinamali* (We have no money, 1983)[237] gives voice to five prisoners, centering on a township rent strike and fiercely decrying informers responsible for the death of strike leader Msizi Dube, while speaking at the same time of the degradation of their own lives. In these activist plays – as in the sphere of poetry at this time – instead of the work being self-contained, the actors often addressed the public directly, making them potential participants in history through the strength of their testimonies, taxing white audience members with the guilt of complicity. At stake for the actors was also the possibility of transforming their own despair through the sheer energy of chanting and dance as well as comic pastiche.

Tooth and Nail (1989),[238] directed by Malcolm Purkey, involved more distance with the audience and great attention to theatrical aesthetic, partly due to the collaboration with Adrian Kohler and Basil Jones's Handspring Puppet Company. Fragmented, surreal, nerve-ridden, the abiding image here is of a rich white madam borne off into the future in a wheelbarrow by her servant, operatically lamenting for her lost property, 'My things! My things!' According to Purkey, life for the cast was sometimes as fragmented as the play itself: 'Our black actors were suddenly engaging with Black Panthers and Black Consciousness of a special American type. They were suddenly forced to question their engagement with all these white intellectuals and playmakers.'[239] In Paul Slabolepszy's play *Mooi Street Moves* (1992),[240] another aspect of a speedily shifting social situation is highlighted: a white country bumpkin enters the wild world of Hillbrow, central Johannesburg, looking for his brother at his last known address, only to find a black, happy-go-lucky huckster who confronts him with his sense of white entitlement, while helping him face a new wild world of gangsters and ruthless property sharks.

Njabulo S Ndebele, writing in 1992, noted the radical tearing of the social fabric around him, describing it as 'nothing less than what in some situations has been called the breakdown of culture'. This, despite all the material progress of 'an over-privileged minority which, in spite of a presence of more than three hundred years, has never shed the mentality of being visitors. Consequently, the fruits of their achievements have no organic connection with the realities of the larger human environment in which they occurred. We have a culture of technical achievement that is merely drifting forward by sheer momentum. Where are we going? We have to do something to rediscover some human direction towards being a nation of the future.'[241]

Some writers, including Ndebele himself, were now taking active steps in this direction. In 1987, Breyten Breytenbach had participated with Frederic van Zyl Slabbert's IDASA (Institute for a Democratic South Africa) in organising a conference in Dakar, Senegal, where exiled ANC members met with influential South Africans to pave the way towards a democratic South Africa.[242] In 1989, Afrikaans poet Antjie Krog participated with Breytenbach in the writers' conference at the Victoria Falls, Zimbabwe, together with other writers who had travelled from South Africa, including André Brink, Etienne van Heerden, Ingrid Winterbach, Ingrid de Kok and Hein Willemse, risking the ire of the apartheid government to meet members of the

ANC in exile. These included poets Mongane Wally Serote (initiator of the liberatory arts foundation Medu Art Ensemble in Botswana, and member of the ANC's London arts and culture desk) and Keorapetse 'Willie' Kgositsile (founding member of the ANC Education, and Arts and Culture departments). 'In front of our very ears the fabric of our country was being spoken into something new,' writes Antjie Krog, 'an unmetallic story, a multicoloured song, sweet and sultry and tolerantly clear.'[243]

It was a time when those who had lived outside the country began writing of the deep effects of return, as in the opening poem of Ingrid de Kok's book *Familiar Ground* (1988):

> To return home, you have to drink its water,
> in a drought, you have to drink its water,
> even from the courtyard well,
> the water blossoming in the gut,
> or brackish, from a burning trough,
> flypaper on your tongue,
> pooling your hands,
> bending when you drink.[244]

At the Victoria Falls conference, the subject of the land came up. 'Since the settlers first settled,' Mongane Wally Serote had written years earlier, 'all their laws and wars have succeeded in only postponing the real issue – that the people want and need their land.'[245] Now Antjie Krog reported one of the black exiles saying, 'When we watched you get off that plane [...] we could tell: that one is a Boer, also that one, not that one. We recognise you, that obsession you have – like us – with the land: it shows, right here between the eyes.'[246] Of the land, Antjie Krog was to write a few years later:

> now you are fought over
> negotiated divided paddocked sold stolen mortgaged
> I want to go underground with you land
> land that would not have me
> land that never belonged to me
> land that I love more fruitlessly than before[247]

Once again, one of the strongest responses to the situation of chaotic transition in South Africa, from the late 1980s to the early 1990s, was to be found in poems that could be read as seismographs of the violent situation. 'A stone against a tank is a stone against a tank/ but a bullet in a child's chest rips into the heart of the house', writes Ingrid de Kok.[248] Robert Berold sees 'In the open space/ inside your heart the bodies lying slaughtered',[249] while Kelwyn Sole hears 'the blood/ crooning/ its vengeance in my ears'.[250]

Denis Hirson

> Tatamkulu Afrika describes being mugged, watching his assailants disappear as he asks himself

> Am I still here,
> stones troubling my spine,
> grass stems sticking in my eyes,
> or does this naked, lonely body run
> with them over the harsh,
> desperate lava of the land?[251]

The body as the locus of the poem, the land torn and unsteady below it, history storming against it: this is a recurring figure of the times, as in the following poem by Karen Press, which remembers the places of power and repression across several decades and reconstitutes them as parts of the body that speaks the poem:

> In that war each of us became the nation:
> the whole nation entered each of us [...]
>
> In Sharpeville your arms died.
> In Uitenhage your tongues died.
> In Boipatong your eyes died.
> In Katlehong and Bekkersdal and Empangeni
>   you died and
> you died and you died.
> That's what I remember.

> In Pretoria your fingers became joint chief of staff.
> In Pretoria your teeth ran the central bank.
> In Pretoria your hair was the president.
> That's what I remember.²⁵²

Just as at this time the country's future lay open, so the act of remembering became crucial, the country's past malleable to exploration and debate. In *Return of the Moon* (1991), Stephen Watson wrote reworked 'versions' of /Xam narratives as told by convicts to the German linguist WH Bleek and his sister-in-law Lucy Lloyd in the 1870s. These narratives in turn remember both the early myths of the /Xam, South Africa's first indigenous people, and the violence of colonisation. One text by the narrator Dia!kwain ends:

> Because
> of this string,
> because of a people
> breaking the string,
> this earth, my place
> is the place
> of something –
> a thing broken –
> that does not
> stop sounding,

breaking within me.[253]

Antjie Krog, in *Lady Anne* (1989) sought links with the eighteenth-century figure of Lady Anne Barnard, who had participated in a time of intense change at the Cape, and bore witness to the debasement of slavery. In the same book, Krog also addresses her own children, telling them that like the sole lying flat at the bottom of the sea they too 'will survive the tide' of transformation that is all around them.[254] Seitlhamo Motsapi, in the poem 'Mushi', first published in 1992, records the movement into the future while looking back with violence at the colonial past (echoing the words of Mqhayi addressed to the Prince of Wales, quoted towards the beginning of the text):

> there is hope yet
> as we feed fire
> into our stride
>
> there is hope yet
> as we remember
> to roll back the blood
> & mutilate the beast
> who brought us mirrors and darkness[255]

The music of the poetry of this time is often lean,

unsettled, open and raw, with 'no time/ for balm', as Joan Metelerkamp puts it in one of her poems.[256] It is a music that asks to be heard aloud, returning to the oral roots of the country's literature. Lesego Rampolokeng begins his poem 'For the Oral' with the lines:

> intuitive it is instructive expressive
> it is excessive flaming it is flailing hand
> knowledge of the age it is rage too hot
> for the page it is searing on the wing
> it is pain on the stage[257]

'It feels like an exciting movement is happening in English poetry in this country: the printed poetry of voice [...] The English language, the language of settlerdom, power and commerce, is being shaped by African sensibilities and forms – African not necessarily meaning black. Increasingly since the 1970s and particularly since the unbanning of the ANC and the demythologisation of Mandela, poets are more and more using the living language, breaking the grids of formal political or literary orthodoxy,'[258] wrote Robert Berold about his 10-year editorship of the review *New Coin*, which more than any other recorded the shift in poetry at this time.

Berold's note of hope from the 1990s, lifting beyond the deep strictures of oppression, is a good conclusion to this account of South African writing, which ends before the first democratic elections of 1994. Several themes have run through these pages, which should give the reader a sense of continuity despite the extreme diversity of origin and form in South African writing, as it has developed since the ninteenth century. These themes include the importance of the oral tradition and the invocation of ancestors, the primacy of relations between people of different races, the involvement of the writer in issues of political power, the emphasis on the symbolic potency of the land, and the material need for land ownership. There is the sense that writing was often an intensely urgent social act, with little place for hermetic abstraction, especially at times of intense political change. Sometimes this writing was informed by religion; often it sought the political conversion of the reader. Only rarely was it able to present South African society, fragmented as it has always been, from several angles at once, or from any great distance.

I am of course aware that there are different versions of this history, that other writers, texts and perspectives might have been highlighted. This survey is intended as no more than a foray into a vast and complex subject, ended at an opportune moment. An account of texts published since 1994 would be different in many ways, and no doubt even more complex, since South African writers are no longer cramped within the confines of a political island where the battle lines were set, but find themselves out in an unpredictable world.

NOTES

1 Denise Coussy, Denis Hirson and Joan Metlerkamp, *Afrique du sud, une traversée littéraire* (Paris: Institut français and Philippe Rey, with a CD produced by the INA, 2011).
2 JM (John Maxwell) Coetzee, *White Writing* (New Haven: Yale University Press, 1988).
3 Nadine Gordimer, *The Black Interpreters* (Johannesburg: Ravan Press, 1973).
4 Njabulo S Ndebele, *Rediscovery of the Ordinary* (Johannesburg: COSAW, 1991).
5 Lieutenant-Colonel Pienaar at the government commission of enquiry into the Sharpeville massacre, quoted in Ambrose Reeves, *Shooting at Sharpeville* (London: Gollancz, 1960), p.95.
6 Gabeba Baderoon, 'Brutus: A memory' in *Safundi: The Journal of South African and American Studies*, Vol. 11, No. 3, July 2010, pp.304–305.
7 There are 11 official languages in South Africa, the percentage of mother-tongue speakers given in brackets according to the 2001 census: IsiZulu (23.8%), IsiXhosa (17.6%), Afrikaans (13.3%), Sepedi (9.4%), Setswana (8.2%), English (8.2%), Sesotho (7.9%), Xitsonga (4.4%), Siswati (2.7%), Tshivenda (2.3%), IsiNdebele (1.6%). The population is divided into 79.2% black, 9.2% white, 9%

coloured, 2.6% Indian.

8 Cited by Njabulo S Ndebele in 'The challenges of the written word: A reflection on prose', in Willem Campschreur and Joost Divenda (eds.), *Culture in Another South Africa* (New York: Olive Branch Press, 1989, online at www.sahistory.org.za).

9 *The Pilgrim's Progress from this world to that which is to come*, written in 1675 by John Bunyan (1628–1688), is an allegorical tale recounting the voyage of Christian from the City of Destruction to the Celestial City of Sion. *Uhambo lo Mhambi* (Lovedale: Missionary Institution Press, 1868) tr. Tiyo Soga (1829–1871).

10 Cited by Njabulo S Ndebele in 'The challenges of the written word: A reflection on prose'.

11 Thomas Mofolo (1877–1948), *Chaka* (Morija: Morija Sesuto Book Depot, 1925); republished tr. Daniel P Kunene (Oxford: Heinemann, 1989), p.167. It is important to note that, as a novelist, Mofolo was not restricted by, or trying to represent, historical fact surrounding Shaka, his life and his reign.

12 Sol T (Solomon Tshekisho) Plaatje (1876–1932), *Boer War Diary* (London: Macmillan, 1901).

13 Sol T Plaatje, *Native Life in South Africa* (London: PS King & Son, 1916); republished 1982 (Johannesburg: Ravan Press, 1982), p.21.

14 Brian Willan, 'Sol T Plaatje and Tswana literature: A preliminary survey' in *Literature and Society in South Africa*, Landeg White and Tim Couzens (eds.) (Cape Town: Longman, 1984).

15 Sol T Plaatje, *Mhudi. An Epic of South African Native Life a Hundred Years Ago* (Alice: Lovedale Press, 1930).

Notes

16 Tim Couzens, Introduction to Sol T Plaatje, *Muhdi* (Oxford: Heinemann, 1989) p.18.
17 Sol T Plaatje, *Mhudi*, pp.154–155.
18 AC (Archibald Campbell) Jordan (1906–1968), *Ingqumbo Yeminyana* (Alice: Lovedale Press, 1940); *The Wrath of the Ancestors*, tr. AC Jordan and Priscilla P Jordan (Alice: Lovedale Press, 1980).
19 SEK (Samuel Edward Krune) Mqhayi (1875–1945), *Imihobe Nemibongo* (Joyous songs and lullabies) (London: Sheldon Press, 1927).
20 The first stanza of 'Nkosi Sikelel' i Afrika' was composed in 1897 by Tembu teacher Enoch Sontonga (c.1860–1904), and first publicly sung in 1899. By 1927, Mqhayi had provided stanzas 2–8. Cf Stephen Gray (ed.), *The Penguin Book of Southern African Verse* (London: Penguin, 1989, p.150).
21 David James Smith, *The Young Mandela* (London: Weidenfeld & Nicolson, 2010), pp.32–33.
22 SEK Mqhayi, 'The Pleiades', tr. Jeff Opland, in Stephen Gray (ed.), *The Penguin Book of Southern African Verse*, pp.148–149. Mqhayi is making oblique reference to the redistribution of land following the First World War.
23 SEK Mqhayi, 'Ah Britain! Great Britain!' in Allan H Findlay (ed.), *Root and Branch: An Anthology of Southern African Literature* (London: Macmillan, 1986), p.98.
24 RRR (Rolfus Reginald Raymond) Dhlomo (1901–1971), *An African Tragedy* (Alice: Lovedale Press, 1928).
25 RRR Dhlomo, 'The Dog Killers' in *The Sjambok*, 18 July 1930, reprinted in Norman Hodge (ed.), *To Kill a Man's Pride* (Johannesburg: Ravan Press, 1984), p.10.
26 William John Burchell (1782–1863), *Travels in the Interior of Southern Africa* (London: Longman, Hurst, Rees, Orme & Brown, 1822).

27 JM Coetzee, 'Reading the South African landscape' in *White Writing* (New Haven: Yale University Press, 1988), p.164. Coetzee's discussion of Burchell is in the essay 'The Picturesque and the South African landscape' in the same volume.
28 Henry Rider Haggard (1856–1925), *Allan Quatermain* (London: Longman, Green, 1887) (www.fullbooks.com/Allan-Quatermain).
29 Thomas Pringle (1789–1834), 'The Caffer Commando', in *African Sketches* (London: Edward Moxon, 1834), pp.58–59.
30 Thomas Pringle, *Narrative of a Residence in South Africa* (London, Edward Moxon, 1834).
31 cf. Die Afrikaanse Taalmuseum en -Monument http://www.golden-arrow.net/wp-content/themes/GOLDEN-ARROW/download/roots_of_afrikaans.pdf. According to this source, the German settlers at the Cape were mainly single men who married Dutch women. French families were purposely spread thinly among the Dutch so that their language would not predominate. As for the slaves, it was important for them to learn Dutch, because only with a knowledge of this language were they allowed to try to buy back their freedom. The same source adds that the first school at the Cape was founded in 1658, so that the children of slaves could learn Dutch. Government language policy leading to the Soweto revolt in 1976 was not without precedent.
32 Sir James Percy FitzPatrick (1862–1931), *Jock of the Bushveld* (London: Longman, Green & Co., 1907).
33 Deneys Reitz (1882–1944), *Commando: A Boer Journal of the Boer War* (London: Faber& Faber, 1929).
34 JM Coetzee, 'Reading the South African landscape', in *White Writing*, p.83.
35 Olive Schreiner (1855–1920), *The Story of an African Farm* (London: Chapman and Hall, 1883); (Harmondsworth:

Penguin, 1982).
36 cf. Nadine Gordimer, 'English-language literature and politics' in *Telling Times, Writing and Living, 1954–2008* (New York: WW Norton & Company, 2010), p.240.
37 Olive Schreiner, *The Story of an African Farm*, 1982, pp.214–215.
38 JM Coetzee, 'Farm novel and plaasroman' in *White Writing*, pp.64–66.
39 Ibid., p.38.
40 cf. 'The farm novels of CM van den Heever' and 'Simple language, simple people: Smith, Paton, Mikro' in JM Coetzee, *White Writing*.
41 Pauline Janet Smith (1882–1959), 'The Pastor's Daughter' in *The Little Karoo* (London: Jonathan Cape, 1925).
42 Christoffel Hermanus Kühn (1903–1968), *Huisies teen die Heuwel* (Cape Town: Nasionale Boekhandel, 1942).
43 Eugène Nielen Marais (1871–1936), *Die Siel van die Mier* (Pretoria: Van Schaik, 1925); *The Soul of the White Ant* tr. Winifred de Kok (London: Methuen, 1937).
44 Eugène Marais, 'Winternag' written under the pseudonym Klaas Vaakie (Sandman), in *Land en Volk*, 23 June 1905; 'Winter Night' tr. John Irons (www.johnirons.blogspot.com/2009/12/winter-poem-in-afrikaans-by-marais.html).
45 Nicholaas Petrus van Wyk Louw (1906–1970), *Die Dieper Reg* (Cape Town: Nationale Pers Beperk, 1938).
46 NP van Wyk Louw, *The Greater Right*, tr. Guy Butler, quoted by JC Kannemeyer in 'NP van Wyk Louw and the Afrikaans Literary Tradition' (http://ifa.amu.edu.pl).
47 Quoted in South African History Online, 'Nicholaas Petrus van Wyk Louw' (www.sahistory.org.za).
48 NP van Wyk Louw, 'Ballade van die Nagtelike Ure' (Ballad of the Night Hours) in *Gestalte en Diere* (Forms and Animals) (Cape Town: Tafelberg, 1942), tr. based on Tony

McGregor, in 'An Afrikaans Love Poem and the end of a love: "Ballade van die Nagtelike Ure" by NP van Wyk Louw' (http://hubpages.com/hub).
49 William Plomer (1903–1973), 'Ula Masondo', *I Speak to Africa* (London: Hogarth Press, 1927) reprinted in *Selected Stories* (Cape Town: David Philip Publishers, 1984), p.80.
50 William Plomer, *Turbott Wolfe* (London: Hogarth Press, 1925).
51 Nadine Gordimer, 'English-language literature and politics' in *Telling Times, Writing and Living, 1954–2008*, p.241.
52 Ignatius Royston Dunnachie (Roy) Campbell (1901–1957), 'On Some South African Novelists', in *Adamastor* (London: Faber & Faber, 1930).
53 Laurens Jan van der Post (1906–1996), *In a Province* (London: The Hogarth Press, 1934, reprinted 1953), p.337.
54 Laurens van der Post, *The Lost World of the Kalahari* (London: The Hogarth Press, 1958).
55 Sarah Gertrude Millin (1889–1968), *God's Stepchildren* (London: Constable Company, 1924).
56 Sarah Gertrude Millin, *King of the Bastards* (New York: Harper, 1949).
57 St J Page Yako (1901–1977), 'Ukufinyezwa nokubiywa komhlaba' in *Umtha Welanga* (Ray of the Sun) (Alice: Lovedale Press, 1958); 'The Contraction and Enclosure of the Land', tr. Robert Kavanagh and ZS Qangule in Robert Kavanagh and ZSQangule (eds.) *The Making of a Servant & other poems* (Johannesburg: Ophir/Ravan Press, 1974).
58 Benedict Wallet Bambatha Vilakazi (1906–1947), 'Ezinkomponi' (On the Gold Mine Compounds) in *Amal'ezulu* (Johannesburg: University of Witwatersrand Press, 1945); 'On the Gold Mines' tr. AC Jordan in Jack Cope and Uys Krige (eds.), *The Penguin Book of South African Verse* (London: Penguin, 1968), pp.300–305.

59 *Jim Comes to Joburg*, 1949, directed by Donald Swanson, featuring Daniel Adnewmah, Dolly Radebe and two jazz groups: the African Inkspots and the Jazz Maniacs.
60 Alan Stewart Paton (1903–1988), *Cry, the Beloved Country* (London: Jonathan Cape, 1944).
61 cf. JM Coetzee, 'Simple language, simple people: Smith, Paton, Mikro' in *White Writing*.
62 Alan Paton, *Cry, the Beloved Country* (London: Penguin, 1966), p.38.
63 Alan Paton, 'Life for a Life' in *Debbie Go Home* (London: Jonathan Cape, 1961).
64 Phyllis Altman (1918–1999), *The Law of the Vultures* (London: Jonathan Cape, 1952), p.186.
65 Solomon Harris (Harry) Bloom (1913–1981), *Episode* (later renamed *Transvaal Episode*) (New York: Doubleday, 1955).
66 Modikwe Dikobe (real name Marks Rammitloa), *The Marabi Dance* (London: Heinemann, 1973), p.75.
67 Peter Abrahams, *Mine Boy* (London: Faber & Faber, 1946), reprinted 1986 (Oxford: Heinemann, 1986), p.10.
68 At the time (1940–1949), the Secretary-General of the ANC was Dr AB Xuma.
69 Peter Abrahams, *Tell Freedom* (London: Faber & Faber, 1954).
70 Ezekiel (Es'kia) Mphahlele (1919–2008), *Down Second Avenue* (London: Faber & Faber, 1959).
71 William (Bloke) Modisane (1923–1986), *Blame Me on History* (London: Thames and Hudson, 1963).
72 Ezekiel Mphahlele, *Down Second Avenue*, reprinted 1971 (London: Faber & Faber, 1971), p.186.
73 Ibid., pp.195–196.
74 Ibid., p.218.
75 Bloke Modisane, *Blame Me on History*, p.190.
76 Lewis Nkosi (1936–2010), cited by Michael Chapman in his

preface to Michael Chapman (ed.), *The Drum Decade* (Pietermaritzburg: University of Natal Press, 1989), p.vii.
77 Lewis Nkosi, 'The fabulous decade – the fifties' in *Home and Exile* (London: Longman, 1965).
78 Nadine Gordimer, *Face to Face* (Johannesburg: Silver Leaf Books, 1949).
79 Nadine Gordimer, *The Lying Days* (New York: Simon & Schuster, 1953).
80 Nadine Gordimer, *A World of Strangers* (London: Gollancz, 1958).
81 Daniel Canodoise (Can) Themba (1924–1968), *The Will to Die* (London: Heinemann, 1972).
82 Alex La Guma (1925–1985), *A Walk in the Night* (Ibadan: Mbari Publications, 1962).
83 Nadine Gordimer, *The Black Interpreters* (Johannesburg: Ravan Press, 1973), p.51.
84 Bartholomeus Jacobus (Bartho) Smit (1924–1986), 'I Take Back My Country' in Denis Hirson (ed.) with Martin Trump, *The Heinemann Book of South African Short Stories* (Oxford: Heinemann, 1994), p.132.
85 Ibid., p.142.
86 Dan Jacobson, *A Dance in the Sun* (London: Weidenfeld & Nicolson, 1956).
87 Dan Jacobson, 'The Zulu and the Zeide' in *The Zulu and the Zeide: Short Stories* (New York: Little, Brown & Company, 1959).
88 Dan Jacobson, *The Beginners* (London: Weidenfeld & Nicolson, 1966).
89 Dan Jacobson, 'Kimberley', in *Time and Time Again* (London: André Deutsch, 1985); (London: Fontana Paperbacks, 1986), pp.8–9.

Notes

90 Herman Charles Bosman (1905–1951), 'Unto Dust ' in *Unto Dust* (Cape Town: Human & Rousseau, 1963; republished 1991), p.18.
91 Herman Charles Bosman, 'A Bekkersdal Marathon' in *Mafeking Road and Other Stories* (Cape Town: Human & Rousseau, 1947).
92 Herman Charles Bosman, *Cold Stone Jug* (Johannesburg: Afrikaanse Persboekhandel, 1949).
93 Herman Charles Bosman, *Cold Stone Jug* (Cape Town: Human & Rousseau, 1999), p.166.
94 Nadine Gordimer, 'Censored, Banned, Gagged' in *The Essential Gesture* (London: Penguin, 1989), p.65.
95 Ruth First, *117 Days* (London: Penguin, 1965).
96 Albie Sachs, *The Jail Diary of Albie Sachs* (London: Harvill Press, 1966).
97 DM Zwelonke, *Robben Island* (London: Heinemann, 1973).
98 Hugh Lewin, *Bandiet* (London: Barrie and Jenkins, 1974).
99 Breyten Breytenbach, *Mouroir: Mirrornotes of a Novel* (Johannesburg: Taurus, 1983).
100 Breyten Breytenbach, 'Propos détenus', afterword to the poetry collection *Feu froid*, tr. Georges-Marie Lory (quote translated into English by Denis Hirson) (Paris: Christian Bourgois, 1983), p.126.
101 Nadine Gordimer, *The Late Bourgeois World* (London: Gollancz, 1966).
102 Alex La Guma, *Stone Country* (Berlin: Seven Seas Publishers, 1967).
103 Alex La Guma, *In the Fog of the Season's End* (London: Heinemann, 1972).
104 Charles Jonathan (Jonty) Driver, *Elegy for a Revolutionary* (London: Faber & Faber, 1969).
105 Robert Knox (Jack) Cope (1913–1991), *The Dawn Comes Twice* (London: Heinemann, 1969).

106 Mary Benson (1919–2000), *At the Still Point* (Boston: Gambit, 1969).
107 Jack Cope, *The Fair House* (London: Macgibbon & Kee, 1955).
108 Jack Cope, 'Flight for Love' in *The Tame Ox* (London: Heinemann, 1960).
109 Ibid.
110 Ezekiel (Es'kia) Mphahlele, *Down Second Avenue*, p.220.
111 Ezekiel (Es'kia) Mphahlele, *The Wanderers* (New York: Macmillan, 1971).
112 Peter Abrahams, *A Wreath for Udomo* (London, Faber & Faber, 1956).
113 Bessie Emery Head (1937–1986), *A Question of Power* (London: Davis-Poynter, 1974).
114 Bessie Head, *The Collector of Treasures and Other Botswana Tales* (Cape Town: David Philip Publishers, 1977), p.101.
115 Dennis Vincent Brutus (1924–2009), 'Nightsong: City' in *Sirens, Knuckles, Boots* (Ibadan: Mbari Publications, 1963).
116 Dennis Brutus, 'To be thrown outward in a steel projectile' in *A Simple Lust* (Oxford: Heinemann, 1973).
117 Arthur Kenneth Nortje (1942–1970), 'Song for a Passport' in Cosmo Pieterse (ed.), *Seven South African Poets* (London: Heinemann, 1971), p.111.
118 Arthur Nortje (1942–1970), 'Waiting' in *Seven South African Poets*, pp.125–126.
119 Ezekiel (Es'kia) Mphahlele, *The African Image* (London, Faber & Faber, 1962), p.109.
120 Adam Small, 'Groot Krismis Gebied' in *Kitaar my Kruis* (Cape Town: HAUM, 1961), tr. Mike Dickman as 'Great Krismis Prayer' in Denis Hirson (ed.), *The Lava of this Land* (Evanston: Northwestern Univesity Press, 1997), p.31.

121 Oswald Joseph Mtshali, 'Sounds of a Cowhide Drum' in *Sounds of a Cowhide Drum* (Johannesburg: Renoster Books, 1971), p.68.
122 Oswald Joseph Mtshali, 'Sunset' in *Sounds of a Cowhide Drum*, p.23.
123 Mongane Wally Serote, 'For Don M – Banned' in *Tsetlo* (Johannesburg: Ad Donker, 1974), p.58.
124 Mongane Wally Serote, 'Hell, Well, Heaven' in *Yakhal'inkomo* (Johannesburg: Ad Donker, 1972), p.25.
125 James Matthews and Gladys Thomas, *Cry Rage* (Johannesburg: Spro-Cas Publications, 1972).
126 Mazisi Raymond Kunene (1930–2006), *Emperor Shaka the Great*, tr. by the author (Oxford: Heinemann, 1979).
127 Ruth Miller, 'The Floating Island' in *Floating Islands* (Cape Town: Human & Rousseau, 1965).
128 Sydney Clouts (1926–1982), 'Poetry is death cast out' in *One Life* (Cape Town: Purnell, 1966).
129 Ingrid Jonker (1933–1965), 'Die kind (wat doodgeskiet is deur soldate by Nyanga)' in *Rook en Oker* (Smoke and Ochre) (Johannesburg: Afrikaanse Pers-Boekhandel, 1963), tr. Jack Cope and William Plomer, in Ingrid Jonker, *Selected Poems* (Cape Town: Human & Rousseau, 1988), p.27.
130 André Brink and JM Coetzee, preface to André Brink and JM Coetzee (eds.), *A Land Apart, A South African Reader* (London: Faber & Faber, 1986), p.9.
131 Quoted in 'Nicholaas Petrus van Wyk Louw', South African History Online (http://www.sahistory.org.za).
132 Stephanus Petrus Daniël le Roux (Etienne Leroux) (1922–1989), *Sewe Dae by die Silbersteins* (Cape Town: Human & Rousseau, 1962); *Seven Days at the Silbersteins*, tr. Charles Eglington (Johannesburg: Central News Agency, 1964).

133 André Brink, *Kennis van die Aand* (Cape Town: Buren Uitgewers, 1973); André Brink, *Looking on Darkness*, tr. by the author (London: WH Allen, 1974).

134 *Race & Class*, Institute of Race Relations, Vol. 16, No. 4, 1975, p.435.

135 André Brink, *'n Droë Wit Seisoen* (Johannesburg: Taurus, 1979), *A Dry White Season*, tr. by the author (London: Vintage, 1998), p.86.

136 André Brink, *'n Oomblik in die Wind* (Johannesburg: Taurus, 1975), *An Instant in the Wind*, tr. by the author, (London: Fontana, 1983), p.79.

137 Breyten Breytenbach, *'n Seisoen in die Paradys* (Johannesburg: Perskor, 1976); *A Season in Paradise*, tr. Rike Vaughan (London: Jonathan Cape, 1980), p.156 (Breytenbach's italics).

138 Breyten Breytenbach, *The True Confessions of an Albino Terrorist* (New York: Farrar Straus Giroux, 1983); (London: Faber & Faber, 1985), p.20.

139 Ibid.

140 Breyten Breytenbach, *A Season in Paradise*, p.98.

141 Breyten Breytenbach, 'ek sal sterf en na my vader gaan' in *'n Seisoen in die Paradys*, p.161, tr. Denis Hirson in *In Africa Even the Flies are Happy* (London, John Calder, 1978), p.77.

142 Adam Small, *Black Bronze Beautiful* (Johannesburg: Ad Donker, 1975), quatrain No. 15.

143 Arthur Nortje, 'Exit Visa' in David Bunn and Jayne Taylor (eds.) *From South Africa* (Chicago: University of Chicago Press, 1988), p.384.

144 Richard Moore Rive (1931–1989), 'Make like slaves' in *Advance, Retreat* (Cape Town: David Philip Publishers, 1983, reprinted 1989), p.84.

145 Ibid., p.92.

146 Achmat Dangor, 'Waiting for Leila' in *Waiting for Leila*

(Johannesburg: Ravan Press, 1981), p.1.
147 Ahmed Essop, *The Visitation* (Johannesburg: Ravan Press, 1980), p.90.
148 Mona Glasser, *King Kong: A Venture in the Theatre* (Cape Town: Norman Howell, 1960), p.60.
149 Gibson Mthuthuzeli Kente (1932–2004), *How Long* (produced in Soweto, 1973); *I Believe* (produced 1974). *Too Late* (produced in Soweto, 1975) is included in Robert Mshengu Kavanagh (ed.) *South African People's Plays* (London: Heinemann, 1981).
150 *S'ketsh'* was founded by Robert McLaren (also known as Robert Mshengu Kavanagh) and co-edited by him until 1975.
151 Gibson Kente, extract from *Too Late* in Allan H Findlay (ed.), *Root and Branch: An Anthology of Southern African Literature*, p.173.
152 *The Classic*, founded by Nat Nakasa in 1963, later became *New Classic*, edited by Sipho Sepamla.
153 Barney Simon (1932–1995), *Jo'burg, Sis* (Johannesburg: Bateleur Press, 1974).
154 Barney Simon interviewed by Garalt MacLiam in *The Star Weekend*, 1986, quoted in eds. Irene Stephanou and Leila Henriques, *The World is an Orange* (Johannesburg: Jacana, 2005), p.7.
155 *No-Good Friday* (1958) and *Nongogo* (1959) are included with *The Coat* (1966) in Athol Fugard, *The Township Plays* (Oxford: Oxford University Press, 1993).
156 Athol Fugard, *The Blood Knot* (Johannesburg: Simondium, 1963).
157 Athol Fugard, *Boesman and Lena* (Cape Town: Buren Publishers, 1969).
158 Athol Fugard, *Hello and Goodbye* (Cape Town: AA Balkema, 1966).

159 Athol Fugard, introduction to *Three Port Elizabeth Plays* (Oxford: Oxford University Press, 1974), p.xi.
160 Athol Fugard, John Kani and Winston Ntshona, *Sizwe Banzi is Dead* and *The Island* (New York: Viking Press, 1974); reprinted with Athol Fugard's *Statements after an Arrest under the Immorality Act* in *Statements: Sizwe Banzi is Dead, The Island* and *Statements after an Arrest under the Immorality Act* (New York: Theatre Communications Group, Inc., 1986), p.75.
161 Robert McLaren, quoted in Anne Fuchs, *Playing the Market* (Amsterdam: Radopi, 2002), p.26.
162 Athol Fugard, *Statements After an Arrest under the Immorality Act*.
163 *Peace and Forgiveness, The Hungry Earth* in Maishe Maponya, *Doing Plays for a Change: Five Works* (Johannesburg: Witwatersrand University Press, 1995).
164 Quoted in Anne Fuchs, *Playing the Market*, p.124.
165 Matsemela Manaka, *Egoli: City of Gold* (Johannesburg: Ravan Press, 1981).
166 Percy Mtwa, Mbongeni Ngema and Barney Simon, *Woza Albert!* (London: Methuen, 1983).
167 Interview with FOSATU Cultural Group, *South African Labour Bulletin*, Vol. 10, No. 8 (July/August 1985), reprinted in David Bunn and Jane Taylor (eds.), *From South Africa*, p.304.
168 Zakes Mda, *We Shall Sing for the Fatherland* (Johannesburg: Ravan Press, 1980).
169 Harold Scheub, Introduction to Nongenile Masithathu Zenani, *The World and the Word* (Wisconsin: The University of Wisconsin Press, 1992), p.19.
170 *Staffrider* editorial, Vol. 1, No.1, 1978, in Andries Oliphant and Ivan Vladislavic (eds.), *Ten Years of Staffrider, 1978–1988* (Johannesburg: Ravan Press, 1988).

Notes

171 Miriam Tlali, *Muriel at Metropolitan* (Johannesburg: Ravan Press, 1975).
172 Mtutuzeli Matshoba, *Call Me not a Man* (Johannesburg: Ravan Press, 1979).
173 Andries Oliphant, 'Turning Point' in *At the End of the Day* (Johannesburg: Justified Press, 1988).
174 Kelwyn Sole, 'The Blood of Our Silence' in *The Blood of Our Silence* (Johannesburg: Ravan Press, 1988), p.122.
175 Chris van Wyk, 'In Detention' in *It's Time to Go Home* (Johannesburg: Ad Donker, 1979), p.45. Cf. Van Wyk's autobiography *Shirley, Goodness and Mercy* (London: Picador, 2006) for more about this poem.
176 Bheki Maseko, 'Mamlambo' in *Staffrider*, Vol. 5, No. 1, 1982. Reprinted in Bheki Maseko, *Mamlambo and Other Stories* (Johannesburg: COSAW, 1991).
177 K Zwide, 'Wooden Spoon' in *Staffrider*, Vol. 2, No. 3, 1979, p.23.
178 Lionel Abrahams (1928–2004), 'The Whiteman Blues' (1974) in Stephen Gray (ed.), *Southern African Verse*, p.273. Aspro is a form of aspirin.
179 Wopko Jensma, 'Spanner in the What? Works' in *I Must Show You my Clippings* (Johannesburg: Ravan Press, 1977).
180 http://www.article19.org/speaking-out/south-africa.
181 Athol Fugard: *A Lesson from Aloes* (Oxford: Oxford University Press, 1981); *Master Harold ... and the Boys* (New York: AA Knopf, 1982).
182 André Brink: *Houd-den-Beck* (Pretoria: Taurus, 1982) tr. by the author as *A Chain of Voices* (London: Faber & Faber, 1982); *Mapmakers: Writing in a State of Siege* (London: Faber & Faber, 1983).
183 Nadine Gordimer in Stephen Clingman (ed.), *The Essential Gesture* (London: Penguin, 1989).

184 Stephen Clingman, *The Novels of Nadine Gordimer: History from the Inside* (Johannesburg: Ravan Press, 1986).
185 Nadine Gordimer, *Burger's Daughter* (London: Jonathan Cape, 1979).
186 Nadine Gordimer, *July's People* (Johannesburg: Ravan Press, 1981).
187 Nadine Gordimer, *The Conservationist* (London: Jonathan Cape, 1974); (Harmondsworth: Penguin Books, 1978), p.266.
188 Ibid., p.267.
189 Stephen Clingman (ed.), *The Essential Gesture*, p.141.
190 JM Coetzee, *Dusklands*, (Johannesburg: Ravan Press, 1974).
191 JM Coetzee, *In the Heart of the Country* (Johannesburg: Ravan Press, 1977).
192 JM Coetzee, *Life & Times of Michael K* (London: Secker &Warburg, 1983).
193 JM Coetzee, *Waiting for the Barbarians* (London: Secker & Warburg, 1980).
194 Stephen Clingman, *The Grammar of Identity* (Oxford: Oxford University Press, 2009), p.221.
195 JM Coetzee, *Foe* (Johannesburg: Ravan Press, 1986).
196 JM Coetzee, *The Age of Iron* (London: Secker & Warburg, 1990), p.102.
197 Karel Schoeman, *Na die Geliefde Land* (Cape Town: Human and Rousseau, 1972); *Promised Land*, tr. Marion V Friedmann (London: Friedmann, 1978).
198 Karel Schoeman, *Afskeid en Vertrek* (Cape Town: Human & Rousseau, 1990); *Take Leave and Go* (London: Sinclair-Stevenson, 1992).
199 Karel Schoeman, *'n Ander Land* (Cape Town: Human & Rousseau, 1984); *Another Country*, tr. David Schalkwyk (London: Sinclair-Stevenson, 1991).

200 Wilma Stockenström, *Die kremetartekspedisie* (Cape Town: Human & Rousseau, 1981); *The Expedition to the Baobab Tree*, tr. JM Coetzee (Johannesburg: Jonathan Ball Publishers, 1983), p.24.
201 Njabulo S Ndebele, 'The Rediscovery of the Ordinary, Some New Writings in South Africa' in Njabulo S Ndebele, *Rediscovery of the Ordinary* (Johannesburg: COSAW, 1991), p.43.
202 Mongane Serote, *To Every Birth its Blood* (Johannesburg: Ravan Press, 1981), p.59.
203 Ibid, p.1.
204 Ibid, p.51.
205 Ibid, p.318.
206 Njabulo S Ndebele, 'The Prophetess' in *Fools and Other Stories* (Harlow: Longman, 1985), p.41.
207 Njabulo S Ndebele, 'Be Gentle' in Denis Hirson (ed.), *The Lava of this Land*, p.75.
208 Njabulo S Ndebele, 'The Prophetess' in Denis Hirson (ed.), *The Lava of this Land*, p.44.
209 Zoë Wicomb, 'A Trip to the Gifberge' in *You Can't Get Lost in Cape Town* (London: Virago, 1987).
210 Ibid.
211 Gcina Mhlophe, 'The Dancer', spoken (and danced) in Marianne Kaplan's film *Songololo* (1989), printed in *Love Child* (Pietermaritzburg: University of KwaZulu-Natal Press, 2002).
212 South African History Online, 'The Campaign for participation in the Tricameral Parliament', http://www.sahistory.org.za/article/campaign-participation-tricameral-parliament.
213 Jeremy Cronin, '"Even Under the Rine of Terror": Insurgent South African Poetry', from *Research in African Literatures*, Vol. 19, No. 1, 1988; reprinted in Jon Cook

(ed.), *Poetry in Theory: An Anthology 1900–2000* (Oxford: Blackwell Publishing, 2004), pp.523–532.
214 Jeremy Cronin, 'To learn how to speak ...' in *Inside* (Johannesburg: Ravan Press, 1983), p.58.
215 Quoted by Ari Sitas in his Introduction to the section 'South African Worker Poets in Struggle' in David Bunn and Jane Taylor (eds.), *From South Africa* (Chicago: University of Chicago Press, 1988), p.275.
216 Mi S'Dumo Hlatshwayo, 'The Black Mamba Rises' in David Bunn and Jane Taylor (eds.), *From South Africa*, p.300. The black mamba is one of the most aggressive and dangerous snakes in the world.
217 Oupa Thando Mthimkulu, 'Out of Africa into Exile', unpublished poem c.1995.
218 Mark Mathabane, *Kaffir Boy* (New York: Macmillan, 1986).
219 Mark Mathabane, *African Women* (New York: HarperCollins, 1994).
220 Sindiwe Magona, *To My Children's Children* (London: The Women's Press, 1991), p.128.
221 Rian Malan, *My Traitor's Heart* (New York: Atlantic Monthly Press, 1990), p.79.
222 Ernst Havemann, 'Bloodsong' in *Bloodsong* (Boston: Houghton Mifflin Company, 1987), (London: Hamish Hamilton, 1988), p.66.
223 Christopher Hope, *White Boy Running* (London: Abacus, 1988), p.261.
224 Christopher Hope, *The Love Songs of Nathan J Swirsky* (London: Macmillan, 1993).
225 Mike Nicol, *The Powers That Be* (London: Bloomsbury, 1990).
226 Ivan Vladislavic, *Missing Persons* (Cape Town: David Philip Publishers, 1989), pp.25–26.

227 Ivan Vladislavic, *The Folly* (Cape Town: David Philip Publishers, 1993), p.123.
228 Nadine Gordimer, *July's People*, opening page.
229 Mark Behr, *Die Reuk van Appels* (Cape Town: Queillerie, 1993); *The Smell of Apples* (London: Abacus, 1995).
230 Nadine Gordimer, *Jump and Other Stories* (London: Bloomsbury, 1991), p.257.
231 Mbongeni Ngema, *Sarafina! The Times, The Man, The Play* (Cape Town: Nasou Via Afrika, 2005).
232 Malcolm Purkey, Introduction to Junction Avenue Theatre Company, *Sophiatown* (Cape Town: David Philip Publishers, 1988), p.ix.
233 Elsa Joubert, *Die Swerfjare van Poppie Nongena* (Cape Town: Tafelberg, 1978); *The Long Journey of Poppie Nongena*, Johannesburg: Jonathan Ball Publishers, 1980).
234 Barney Simon, *Born in the RSA: Four workshopped plays* (Johannesburg: Witwatersrand University Press, 1997).
235 Percy Mtwa, *Bopha!* in Duma Ndlovu (ed.), *Woza Afrika! An Anthology of South African Plays* (New York: George Braziller, 1986).
236 *Wathint' abafazi, wathint' imbokodo* in *More Market Plays*, selected by John Kani (Johannesburg: Ad Donker, 1994), cf. Anne Fuchs, *Playing the Market*, pp.130–132.
237 Mbongeni Ngema, *Asinamali* in Duma Ndlovu (ed.), *Woza Afrika! An Anthology of South African Plays*.
238 *Tooth and Nail* in Martin Orkin (ed.), *At the Junction: Four plays by the Junction Avenue Theatre Company* (Johannesburg: Witwatersrand University Press, 1989).
239 Kerry Bystrom, 'Culture and politics after apartheid: views from the Market Theatre – an interview with Malcolm Purkey' in *Safundi: The Journal of South African and American Studies*, Vol. 11, No. 3, July 2010, p.203.

240 Paul Slabolepszy, *Mooi Street and Other Moves* (Johannesburg: Witwatersrand University Press, 1994).
241 Njabulo S Ndebele, 'Recovering Childhood' in Njabulo S Ndebele, *Fine Lines from the Box* (Johannesburg: Umuzi, 2007), pp.42–43.
242 Mark Gevisser, *A Legacy of Liberation: Thabo Mbeki and the future of the South African dream* (New York: Palgrave Macmillan, 2009), pp.193–196.
243 Antjie Krog, *A Change of Tongue* (Johannesburg: Random House, 2003), p.168.
244 Ingrid de Kok, 'To drink its water' in *Familiar Ground* (Johannesburg: Ravan Press, 1988), p.10.
245 Mongane Serote, *To Every Birth its Blood*, p.327.
246 Antjie Krog, *A Change of Tongue*, p.168.
247 Antjie Krog, 'land' in *Gedigte 1989–1995* (Cape Town: Human & Rousseau, 1995), tr. Karen Press in *Down to My Last Skin* (Johannesburg: Random House, 2000), p.114.
248 Ingrid de Kok, 'Al wat kind is' in *Familiar Ground* (Johannesburg: Ravan Press, 1988), p.59.
249 Robert Berold, 'Dark City' in *The Fires of the Dead* (Cape Town: The Carrefour Press, 1989), p.44.
250 Kelwn Sole, 'Motherland' in *The Blood of Our Silence*, p.60.
251 Tatamkulu Afrika, 'The Mugging' in *Dark Rider* (Cape Town: Snailpress, 1992), p.35.
252 Karen Press, 'Tiresias in the City of Heroes' in *Home* (Manchester: Carcanet Press, 2000).
253 Stephen Watson (1954–2011), version of narrative by Dia!kwain, 'Song of the Broken String', in *Return of the Moon* (Cape Town: The Carrefour Press, 1991), pp.59–60.
254 Antjie Krog, 'transparent van die tongvis' in *Lady Anne* (Johannesburg: Taurus, 1990), p.92; tr. Denis Hirson as 'Transparency of the Sole' in Denis Hirson (ed.), *The Lava of this Land*, p.217.

Notes

255 Seitlhamo Motsapi, 'mushi', in *earthstepper/ the ocean is very shallow* (Grahamstown: Deep South, 2003), p.43.
256 Joan Metelerkamp, 'Sunday Night – On my Own – After the Uitenhage Shootings' in *Signs*, collections of poetry by Francis Faller, Sally-Anne Murray and Joan Metelerkamp (Cape Town: The Carrefour Press, 1992), p.98.
257 Lesego Rampolokeng, 'For the Oral' in *Talking Rain* (Johannesburg: COSAW, 1993), p.37.
258 Robert Berold, 'On editing a poetry magazine' in *Comment*, No. 10, Summer 1992, pp.7–8.

BIBLIOGRAPHY

Note: Books listed here correspond to the most recent editions cited in the text (in the Notes section there are references to first editions). Where a work has been translated into English, the translated work is cited.

Afrikaanse Taalmuseum en -Monument, http://www.golden-arrow.net/wp-content/themes/GOLDEN-ARROW/download/roots_of_afrikaans.pdf.

Altman, Phyllis, *The Law of the Vultures* (London, Jonathan Cape, 1952).

Abrahams, Peter, *Mine Boy* (Oxford: Heinemann, 1986).

Abrahams, Peter, *Tell Freedom* (London: Faber & Faber, 1954).

Abrahams, Peter, *A Wreath for Udomo* (London: Faber & Faber, 1956).

Afrika, Tatamkulu, *Dark Rider* (Cape Town: Snailpress, 1992).

Baderoon, Gabeba, 'Brutus: A memory' in *Safundi: The Journal of South African and American Studies*, Vol. 11, No. 3, July 2010.

Behr, Mark, *The Smell of Apples* (London: Abacus, 1995).

Benson, Mary, *At the Still Point* (Boston: Gambit, 1969).

Berold, Robert, *The Fires of the Dead* (Cape Town: The Carrefour Press, 1989).

Berold, Robert, 'On editing a poetry magazine' in *Comment*, No. 10, Summer 1992.

Bloom, Harry, *Episode* (later renamed *Transvaal Episode*) (New York: Doubleday, 1955).

Bosman, Herman Charles, *Mafeking Road and Other Stories* (Cape Town: Human & Rousseau, 1947).

Bosman, Herman Charles (1905–1951), *Unto Dust* (Cape Town: Human & Rousseau, 1991).

Bosman, Charles Herman, *Cold Stone Jug* (Cape Town: Human & Rousseau, 1999).

Breytenbach, Breyten, *A Season in Paradise*, tr. Rike Vaughan (London: Jonathan Cape, 1980).

Breyten Breytenbach, *In Africa Even the Flies are Happy*, tr. Denis Hirson (London: John Calder, 1978).

Breytenbach, Breyten, *Mouroir: Mirrornotes of a Novel* (Johannesburg: Taurus, 1983).

Breytenbach, Breyten, 'Propos détenus', Afterword to Breytenbach, Breyten, *Feu froid* (Cold Fire), tr. Georges-Marie Lory (Paris: Christian Bourgois, 1983).

Breytenbach, Breyten, *The True Confessions of an Albino Terrorist* (London: Faber & Faber, 1985).

Brink, André, *Looking on Darkness* (London: WH Allen, 1974).

Brink, André, *A Chain of Voices* (Pretoria: Taurus, 1982).

Brink, André, *An Instant in the Wind* (London: Fontana, 1983).

Brink, André, *Mapmakers: Writing in a State of Siege* (London: Faber & Faber, 1983).

Brink, André, *A Dry White Season* (London: Vintage, 1998).

Brink, André and Coetzee, JM (eds.), *A Land Apart: A South African Reader* (London: Faber & Faber, 1986).

Brutus, Dennis, *Sirens, Knuckles, Boots* (Ibadan: Mbari Publications, 1963).

Brutus, Dennis, *A Simple Lust* (Oxford: Heinemann, 1973).

Bunn, David and Taylor, Jayne, (eds.), *From South Africa* (Chicago: University of Chicago Press, 1988).

Bunyan, John, *Uhambo lo Mhambi* (The Pilgrim's Progress from this world to that which is to come) tr. Tiyo Soga (Lovedale: Missionary Institution Press, 1868).

Burchell, William J, *Travels in the Interior of Southern Africa* (London: Longman, Hurst, Rees, Orme and Brown, 1822).

Bystrom, Kerry, 'Culture and politics after apartheid: views from the Market Theatre – an interview with Malcolm Purkey' in *Safundi: The Journal of South African and American Studies*, Vol. 11, No. 3, July 2010.

Campbell, Roy, *Adamastor* (London: Faber & Faber, 1930).

Clingman, Stephen, *The Novels of Nadine Gordimer: History from the Inside* (Johannesburg: Ravan Press, 1986).

Clingman, Stephen, *The Grammar of Identity* (Oxford: Oxford University Press, 2009).

Clouts, Sydney, *One Life* (Cape Town: Purnell, 1966).

Chapman, Michael, Preface to Chapman, Michael (ed.), *The Drum Decade* (Pietermaritzburg: University of Natal Press, 1989).

Coetzee, JM, *Dusklands* (Johannesburg: Ravan Press, 1974).

Coetzee, JM, *In the Heart of the Country* (Johannesburg: Ravan Press, 1977).

Coetzee, JM, *Life & Times of Michael K* (London: Secker & Warburg, 1983).

Coetzee, JM, *Foe* (Johannesburg: Ravan Press, 1986).

Coetzee, JM, *The Age of Iron* (London: Secker & Warburg, 1990).

Coetzee, JM, *Waiting for the Barbarians* (London: Secker & Warburg, 1980).

Coetzee, JM, *White Writing* (New Haven: Yale University Press, 1988).

Cope, Jack, *The Fair House* (London: Macgibbon & Kee, 1955).

Cope, Jack, *The Tame Ox* (London: Heinemann, 1960).

Cope, Jack, *The Dawn Comes Twice* (London: Heinemann, 1969).

Cope, Jack and Krige, Uys (eds.), *The Penguin Book of South African Verse* (London: Penguin, 1968).

Coussy, Denise; Hirson, Denis and Metelerkamp, Joan, *Afrique du sud, une traversée littéraire* (Paris: Institut français and Philippe Rey, CD produced by the INA, 2011).

Couzens, Tim, Introduction to Plaatje, Sol T, *Mubdi* (Oxford: Heinemann, 1989).

Cronin, Jeremy, *Inside* (Johannesburg: Ravan Press, 1983).

Cronin, Jeremy, '"Even Under the Rine of Terror": Insurgent South African Poetry', in Jon Cook (ed.), *Poetry in Theory: An Anthology 1900–2000* (Oxford: Blackwell Publishing, 2004).

Dangor, Achmat, *Waiting for Leila* (Johannesburg: Ravan Press, 1981).

De Kok, Ingrid, *Familiar Ground* (Johannesburg: Ravan Press, 1988).

Dhlomo, RRR, *An African Tragedy* (Alice: Lovedale Press, 1928).

Dhlomo, RRR, 'The Dog Killers' in Hodge, Norman (ed.), *To Kill a Man's Pride* (Johannesburg: Ravan Press, 1984).

Dikobe, Modikwe (Marks Rammitloa), *The Marabi Dance* (London: Heinemann, 1973).

Driver, Jonty, *Elegy for a Revolutionary* (London: Faber & Faber, 1969).

Essop, Ahmed *The Visitation* (Johannesburg: Ravan Press, 1980).

Faller, Francis; Murray, Sally-Anne; and Metelerkamp, Joan, *Signs* (Cape Town: The Carrefour Press, 1992).

Findlay, Allan H (ed.), *Root and Branch: An Anthology of Southern African Literature* (London: Macmillan, 1986).

First, Ruth, *117 Days* (London: Penguin, 1965).

FitzPatrick, Sir Percy, *Jock of the Bushveld* (London: Longman, Green & Co, 1907).

Fuchs, Anne, *Playing the Market* (Amsterdam: Radopi, 2002).

Fugard, Athol, *The Township Plays* (Oxford: Oxford University Press, 1993).

Fugard, Athol, *The Blood Knot* (Johannesburg: Simondium, 1963).

Fugard, Athol, *Hello and Goodbye* (Cape Town: AA Balkema, 1966).

Fugard, Athol, *Boesman and Lena* (Cape Town: Buren

Publishers, 1969).

Fugard, Athol, *Three Port Elizabeth Plays* (Oxford: Oxford University Press, 1974).

Fugard, Athol, *A Lesson from Aloes* (Oxford: Oxford University Press, 1981).

Fugard, Athol, *Master Harold ... and the Boys* (New York: AA Knopf, 1982).

Fugard, Athol; Kani, John, and Ntshona, Winston, *Statements: Sizwe Banzi is Dead, The Island*, and *Statements After an Arrest under the Immorality Act* (New York: Theatre Communications Group, Inc., 1986).

Gevisser, Mark, *A Legacy of Liberation: Thabo Mbeki and the future of the South African dream* (New York: Palgrave Macmillan, 2009).

Glasser, Mona, *King Kong: A Venture in the Theatre* (Cape Town: Norman Howell, 1960).

Gordimer, Nadine, *The Black Interpreters* (Johannesburg: Ravan Press, 1973).

Gordimer, Nadine, *Face to Face* (Johannesburg: Silver Leaf Books, 1949).

Gordimer, Nadine, *The Lying Days* (New York: Simon & Schuster, 1953).

Gordimer, Nadine, *A World of Strangers* (London: Gollancz, 1958).

Gordimer, Nadine, *The Black Interpreters* (Johannesburg: Ravan Press, 1973).

Gordimer, Nadine, *The Late Bourgeois World* (London: Gollancz, 1966).

Gordimer, Nadine, *The Essential Gesture* (London: Penguin, 1989).

Gordimer, Nadine, *Burger's Daughter* (London: Jonathan Cape, 1979).

Gordimer, Nadine, *July's People* (Johannesburg: Ravan Press, 1981).

Gordimer, Nadine, *The Conservationist* (Harmondsworth: Penguin Books, 1978).

Gordimer, Nadine, *Jump and Other Stories* (London: Bloomsbury, 1991).

Gordimer, Nadine, *Telling Times, Writing and Living, 1954–2008* (New York: WW Norton & Company, 2010).

Gray, Stephen (ed.), *The Penguin Book of Southern African Verse* (London: Penguin, 1989).

Haggard, Sir Rider, *Allan Quatermain* (London: Longman, Green, 1887).

Havemann, Ernst, *Bloodsong*, (London: Hamish Hamilton, 1988).

Head, Bessie, *A Question of Power* (London: Davis-Poynter, 1974).

Head, Bessie, *The Collector of Treasures and Other Botswana Tales* (Cape Town: David Philip Publishers, 1977).

Hirson, Denis with Trump, Martin (eds.), *The Heinemann Book of South African Short Stories* (Oxford: Heinemann, 1994).

Hirson, Denis (ed.), *The Lava of this Land* (Evanston: Northwestern University Press, 1997).

Hope, Christopher, *White Boy Running* (London: Abacus, 1988).

Hope, Christopher, *The Love Songs of Nathan J Swirsky* (London: Macmillan, 1993).

Irons, John http://johnirons.blogspot.com/2009/12/winter-poem-in-afrikaans-by-marais.html.

Jacobson, Dan, *A Dance in the Sun* (London: Weidenfeld & Nicolson, 1956).

Jacobson, Dan, *The Zulu and the Zeide; Short Stories* (New York: Little, Brown & Company, 1959).

Jacobson, Dan, *The Beginners* (London: Weidenfeld & Nicolson, 1966).

Jacobson, Dan, *Time and Time Again* (London: Fontana Paperbacks, 1986).

Jensma, Wopko, *I Must Show You My Clippings* (Johannesburg: Ravan Press, 1977).

Jonker, Ingrid, *Selected Poems*, tr. Jack Cope and William Plomer (Cape Town: Human & Rousseau, 1988).

Jordan, AC, *The Wrath of the Ancestors*, tr. AC Jordan and Priscilla P Jordan (Alice: Lovedale Press, 1980).

Joubert, Elsa, *The Long Journey of Poppie Nongena* (Johannesburg: Jonathan Ball Publishers, 1980).

Kani, John, *More Market Plays* (selected by John Kani) (Johannesburg: Ad Donker, 1994).

Kannemeyer, JC, 'NP van Wyk Louw and the Afrikaans Literary Tradition', http://ifa.amu.edu.pl.

Kavanagh, Robert (Robert McLaren) and Qangule, ZS (eds. and tr.), *The Making of a Servant & other poems* (Johannesburg: Ophir/Ravan Press, 1974).

Kavanagh, Robert Mshengu (Robert McLaren) (ed.), *South African People's Plays* (London: Heinemann, 1981).

Krog, Antjie, *Lady Anne* (Johannesburg: Taurus, 1990).

Krog, Antjie, *Down to My Last Skin* (Johannesburg: Random House, 2000).

Krog, Antjie, *A Change of Tongue* (Johannesburg: Random House, 2003).

Kunene, Mazisi, *Emperor Shaka the Great*, tr. by the author (Oxford: Heinemann, 1979).

La Guma, Alex, *A Walk in the Night* (Ibadan: Mbari Publications, 1962).

La Guma, Alex, *Stone Country* (Berlin: Seven Seas Publishers, 1967).

La Guma, Alex, *In the Fog of the Season's End* (London: Heinemann, 1972).

Leroux, Etienne, *Seven Days at the Silbersteins*, tr. Charles Eglington (Johannesburg: Central News Agency, 1964).

Lewin, Hugh, *Bandiet* (London: Barrie and Jenkins, 1974).

Louw, NP van Wyk, *Die Dieper Reg* (Cape Town: Nationale Pers Beperk, 1938).

Louw, NP van Wyk, *Gestalte en Diere* (Cape Town: Tafelberg, 1942).

Magona, Sindiwe, *To My Children's Children* (London: The Women's Press, 1991).

Malan, Rian, *My Traitor's Heart* (New York: Atlantic Monthly Press, 1990).

Manaka, Matsemela, *Egoli: City of Gold* (Johannesburg: Ravan Press, 1981).

Maponya, Maishe, *Doing Plays for a Change: Five Works* (Johannesburg: Witwatersrand University Press, 1995).

Marais, Eugène, *The Soul of the White Ant* tr. from the Afrikaans by Winifred de Kok (London: Methuen, 1937).

Maseko, Bheki, *Mamlambo and Other Stories* (Johannesburg: COSAW, 1991).

Mathabane, Mark, *Kaffir Boy* (New York: Macmillan, 1986).

Mathabane, Mark, *African Women* (New York: HarperCollins, 1994).

Matshoba, Mtutuzeli, *Call Me not a Man* (Johannesburg: Ravan Press, 1979).

Matthews, James and Thomas, Gladys, *Cry Rage* (Johannesburg: Spro-Cas Publications, 1972).

McGregor, Tony, 'An Afrikaans Love Poem and the end of a love: Ballade van die Nagtelike Ure by NP van Wyk Louw', http://hubpages.com/hub.

Mda, Zakes, *We Shall Sing for the Fatherland* (Johannesburg: Ravan Press, 1980).

Mhlophe, Gcina, *Love Child* (Pietermaritzburg: University of KwaZulu-Natal Press, 2002)

Mikro (Kühn, CH), *Huisies Teen die Heuwel* (Cape Town: Nasionale Boekhandel, 1942).

Miller, Ruth, *Floating Islands* (Cape Town: Human & Rousseau, 1965).

Millin, Sarah Gertrude, *God's Stepchildren* (London: Constable

Company, 1924).

Millin, Sarah Gertrude, *King of the Bastards* (New York: Harper, 1949).

Modisane, Bloke, *Blame Me on History* (London: Thames and Hudson, 1963).

Mofolo, Thomas, *Chaka* tr. Daniel P Kunene (Oxford: Heinemann, 1989).

Motsapi, Seitlhamo, *earthstepper/ the ocean is very shallow*, (Grahamstown: Deep South, 2003).

Mphahlele, Ezekiel (Es'kia), *Down Second Avenue* (London: Faber & Faber, 1971).

Mphahlele, Ezekiel (Es'kia), *The African Image* (London: Faber & Faber, 1962).

Mphahlele, Ezekiel (Es'kia), *The Wanderers* (New York: Macmillan, 1971).

Mqhayi, SEK, *Imihobe Nemibongo* (London: Sheldon Press, 1927).

Mthimkulu, Oupa Thando, 'Out of Africa into Exile', unpublished poem c.1995.

Mtshali, Oswald, *Sounds of a Cowhide Drum* (Johannesburg: Renoster Books, 1971).

Mtwa, Percy; Ngema, Mbongeni and Simon, Barney, *Woza Albert!* (London: Methuen, 1983).

Ndebele, Njabulo S, *Fools and Other Stories* (Harlow: Longman, 1985).

Ndebele, Njabulo S, 'The challenges of the written word: A reflection on prose' in Campschreur, Willem and Divenda, Joost (eds.), *Culture in Another South Africa* (New York: Olive Branch Press, 1989).

Ndebele, Njabulo S, *Rediscovery of the Ordinary* (Johannesburg: COSAW, 1991).

Ndebele, Njabulo S, *Fine Lines from the Box* (Johannesburg: Umuzi, 2007).

Ndlovu, Duma (ed.), *Woza Afrika! An Anthology of South African*

Plays (New York: George Braziller, 1986).
Ngema, Mbongeni, *Sarafina! The Times, The Man, The Play* (Cape Town: Nasou Via Afrika, 2005).
Nicol, Mike, *The Powers That Be* (London: Bloomsbury, 1990).
Nkosi, Lewis, *Home and Exile* (London: Longman, 1965).
Oliphant, Andries, *At the End of the Day* (Johannesburg: Justified Press, 1988).
Oliphant, Andries and Vladislavic, Ivan (eds.), *Ten Years of Staffrider, 1978–1988* (Johannesburg: Ravan Press, 1988).
Orkin, Martin (ed.), *At the Junction: Four plays by the Junction Avenue Theatre Company* (Johannesburg: Witwatersrand University Press, 1989).
Paton, Alan, *Cry, the Beloved Country* (London: Penguin, 1966).
Paton, Alan, *Debbie Go Home* (London: Jonathan Cape, 1961).
Pieterse, Cosmo (ed.), *Seven South African Poets* (London: Heinemann, 1971).
Plaatje, Sol T, *Boer War Diary* (London: Macmillan, 1901).
Plaatje, Sol T, *Native Life in South Africa*, (Johannesburg: Ravan Press, 1982).
Plaatje, Sol T, *Mhudi: An Epic of South African Native Life a Hundred Years Ago* (Alice: Lovedale Press, 1930).
Plomer, William, *Turbott Wolfe* (London: The Hogarth Press, 1925).
Plomer, William, *Selected Stories* (Cape Town: David Philip Publishers, 1984).
Press, Karen, *Home* (Manchester: Carcanet, 2000).
Pringle, Thomas, *African Sketches* (London: Edward Moxon, 1834).
Pringle, Thomas, *Narrative of a Residence in South Africa* (London: Edward Moxon, 1834).
Purkey, Malcolm, Introduction to Junction Avenue Theatre Company, *Sophiatown* (Cape Town: David Philip Publishers, 1988).

Bibliography

Race & Class, Institute of Race Relations, Vol. 16, No. 4, 1975.

Rampolokeng, Lesego, *Talking Rain* (Johannesburg: COSAW, 1993).

Reeves, Ambrose, *Shooting at Sharpeville* (London: Gollancz, 1960).

Reitz, Deneys, *Commando: A Boer Journal of the Boer War* (London: Faber & Faber, 1929).

Rive, Richard, *Advance, Retreat* (Cape Town: David Philip Publishers, 1989).

Sachs, Albie, *The Jail Diary of Albie Sachs* (London: Harvill Press, 1966).

Scheub, Harold, Introduction to Zenani, Nongenile Masithathu, *The World and the Word* (Wisconsin: The University of Wisconsin Press, 1992).

Schoeman, Karel, *Promised Land*, tr. Marion V Friedmann (London: Friedmann, 1978).

Schoeman, Karel, *Another Country* tr. David Schalkwyk (London: Sinclair-Stevenson, 1991).

Schoeman, Karel, *Take Leave and Go* (London: Sinclair-Stevenson, 1992).

Schreiner, Olive, *The Story of an African Farm* (Harmondsworth: Penguin, 1982).

Serote, Mongane Wally, *Tsetlo* (Johannesburg: Ad Donker, 1974).

Serote, Mongane Wally, *Yakhal'inkomo* (Johannesburg: Ad Donker, 1972).

Serote, Mongane, *To Every Birth its Blood* (Johannesburg: Ravan Press, 1981).

Simon, Barney, *Jo'burg, Sis* (Johannesburg: Bateleur Press, 1974).

Simon, Barney, *Born in the RSA: Four Workshopped Plays* (Johannesburg: Witwatersrand University Press, 1997).

Sitas, Ari, Introduction to 'South African Worker Poets in Struggle' in Bunn, David and Taylor, Jane (eds.), *From South Africa* (Chicago: University of Chicago Press, 1988).

Slabolepszy, Paul, *Mooi Street and Other Moves* (Johannesburg: Witwatersrand University Press, 1994).

Small, Adam, *Kitaar my Kruis*, (Cape Town: HAUM, 1961).

Small, Adam, *Black Bronze Beautiful* (Johannesburg: Ad Donker, 1975).

Smith, David James, *The Young Mandela* (London: Weidenfeld & Nicolson, 2010).

Smith, Pauline, *The Little Karoo* (London: Jonathan Cape, 1925).

Sole, Kelwyn, *The Blood of Our Silence* (Johannesburg: Ravan Press, 1988).

South African History Online, 'Nicholaas Petrus van Wyk Louw' http://www.sahistory.org.za.

South African History Online, 'The Campaign for participation in the Tricameral Parliament' http://www.sahistory.org.za/article/campaign-participation- tricameral-parliament.

'Speaking out for Free Expression 1987–2007 and beyond' http://www.article19.org/speaking-out/south-africa.

Stephanou, Irene and Henriques, Leila, *The World is an Orange* (Johannesburg: Jacana, 2005).

Stockenström, Wilma, *The Expedition to the Baobab Tree*, tr. JM Coetzee (Johannesburg: Jonathan Ball Publishers, 1983).

Themba, Can, *The Will to Die* (London: Heinemann, 1972).

Tlali, Miriam, *Muriel at Metropolitan* (Johannesburg: Ravan Press, 1975).

Van der Post, Laurence, *In a Province* (London: The Hogarth Press, 1953).

Van der Post, Laurens, *The Lost World of the Kalahari* (London: The Hogarth Press, 1958).

Van Wyk, Chris, *It's Time to Go Home* (Johannesburg: Ad Donker, 1979).

Van Wyk, Chris, *Shirley, Goodness and Mercy* (London: Picador, 2006).

Vilakazi, BWB (1906–1947), *Amal'ezulu* (Johannesburg:

Witwatersrand University Press, 1945).
Vladislavic, Ivan, *Missing Persons* (Cape Town: David Philip Publishers, 1989).
Vladislavic, Ivan, *The Folly* (Cape Town: David Philip Publishers, 1993).
Watson, Stephen, *Return of the Moon* (Cape Town: The Carrefour Press, 1991).
Wicomb, Zoë, *You Can't Get Lost in Cape Town* (London: Virago, 1987).
Willan, Brian, 'Sol T Plaatje and Tswana literature: A preliminary survey' in White, Landeg and Couzens, Tim (eds.), *Literature and Society in South Africa* (Cape Town: Longman, 1984).
Zwelonke, DM, *Robben Island* (London: Heinemann, 1973).

INDEX

A
Abrahams, Lionel 69
Abrahams, Peter 30-31, 41
Ad Donker Publishers 46
Adnewmah, Daniel 107n
African Inkspots 107n
African National Congress (ANC) 3, 9, 39, 44, 64, 72, 81, 84, 91, 97
    Education, and Arts and Culture departments 92
African Resistance Movement 39
Afrika, Tatamkulu 94,
Afrikaans 16, 19-22, 49
    medium of instruction 63
    official language 101n
    poetry 20
    poets 49, 69, 91
    writing 45, 56
Afrikaanse Taalmuseum en -Monument, Die 104n
Afrikaner
    populism 27
    writers 50
Altman, Phyllis 29-30
Anglican Church 44
Antigone 62
Anti-Slavery Society 16
apartheid 5-6, 26-27, 32-33, 41, 52-53, 58-59, 64, 66, 70, 84-86, 91
Asvat, Farouk 66

B

Baderoon, Gabeba 5
Bambatha Rebellion 8, 10, 40
Bantu Men's Social Centre 60
Baralong 9
Barberton Gold Fields News 17
Barnard, Chris 51
Barnard, Lady Anne 96
Becket, Samuel 61
Behr, Mark 87
Benson, Mary 40
Berold, Robert ix, 93, 97-98
Biko, Steve 70
Black Consciousness 55, 63, 65, 70, 72, 90
black
    poetry 49
    poets 46
    population 101n
    -white relations 25
    writing 13, 29, 31, 35
Black Sash 44
Bleek, WH 95
Bloom, Harry 30, 58
Boer Republics 16
Boers 2, 9, 80
Bolt 86
Bosman, Herman Charles 37, 38, 39
Botha, PW 83-84
Botswana 41, 42, 92
boycotts
    consumer 80
    South African theatre 61-62
Breytenbach, Breyten 51, 53-55, 91
Brink, André 51, 52-53, 71, 91
British
    settlers 15
    writers 14
Brutus, Dennis 5, 42-43
Bryceland, Yvonne 63
Bunyan, John 7
Burchell, William J 14
Butler, Guy 49

Index

C
Campbell, Roy 24, 25-26
Carnegie Commission 19
Catholic Church 44
Celliers, Jan FE 20
Citashe, IWW 6-7
Classic, The 60, 113n
Clingman, Stephen ix, 71
Cloete, Stuart 17
Clouts, Sydney 49
Coetzee, JM ix, 14, 71, 73-75
coloured/s 2, 80
    Cape 45
    communities 81
    farm workers 20
    identity 56
    male 57
    population 2, 101n-102n
    writers 56
Congress Alliance 32
Contrast 40
Cope, Jack 40, 41
Coussy, Denise vii
Cronin, Jeremy 81-82
Cuban soldiers 83

D
Dangor, Achmat 56, 57, 66
David Philip Publishers 46
De Klerk, FW 3, 84
De Kok, Ingrid 91, 92, 93
De Vries, Abraham 51
Dertigers, Die (Writers of the thirties) 21
Dhlamini, Ezekiel 58
Dhlomo, RRR 13, 23
Dia!kwain 95
Dikobe, Modikwe 30
Dockworkers strike 55
Doyle, Arthur Conan 17
Driver, CJ 40
Drum 32-33, 34, 35, 58
Du Toit, JD (Totius) 20

Denis Hirson

Dutch House of Orange 16
Dutch Reformed Church 52

E
elections
  1984 81
  1987 85
  1994 98
English
  language 7, 97
  official language 19
  playwrights 62
  poetry 97
  poets 14, 49
  writing/writers 46, 69
Essop, Ahmed 57-58, 66, 113n
Everyman 63
exile 44, 46, 65, 78, 84, 92
  poets in 42-43

F
farm novel, *see* plaasroman
FIFA World Cup 1, 4-5
First, Ruth 39
Fischer, Bram 71
FitzPatrick, James Percy 17
Flame of Civilisation 2
Freedom Charter 32
French Morija Mission 8
Fugard, Athol 60-62, 63, 71

G
Glenn, Ian 86
Gordimer, Nadine ix, 33-35, 40, 41, 71, 72, 73, 87, 88
Gottschalk, Keith 82
Gramsci, Antonio 87
Great Trek 17, 22
Grotowski, Jerzy 61
Gwala, Mafika 46, 66

H
Haggard, Henry Rider 14-15
Handspring Puppet Company 90

Havemann, Ernst 85
Head, Bessie 41-42
Hlatshwayo, Mi S'Dumo 65, 82-83
Hogarth Press 23
Hope, Christopher 85-86
Horn, Peter 82
Huisgenoot 36

I
iimbongi 11
immigration 37
Immorality Act 52, 63
Imperial Light Horse Regiment 17
Imvo Zabantsundu (African Opinion) 7
Indian/s 2, 57, 80-81
    population 101n
Institute for a Democratic South Africa (IDASA) 91
Iron, Ralph *see* Schreiner, Olive
IsiNdebele 101n
IsiXhosa 101n
IsiZulu 101n

J
Jabavu, John Tengo 7
Jacobson, Dan 36-37
Jameson Raid 17
Jazz Maniacs 107n
Jensma, Wopko 69-70
Jim Comes to Joburg 28
Johannesburg 27, 29-30, 47
Jones, Basil 90
Jonker, Ingrid 49, 50
Jordan, AC 8, 10-11
Joubert, Elsa 88-89
Junction Avenue Theatre Company 88

K
Kani, John 62, 63
Kaplan, Marianne 117n
Kente, Gibson Mthuthuzeli 58-60, 64
Kgositsile, Keorapetse 'Willie' 90, 92
Khoikhoi 26, 78
King William's Town 7

141

Kirkwood, Mike 65
Klaas Vaakie (Sandman) 105n
Klotz, Phyllis 89
Kohler, Adrian 90
Kotze, Sandra 88
Krige, Uys 49
Krog, Antjie 91, 93, 96
Kruger, Rayn 17
Kühn, CH (Mikro) 2
Kunene, Mazisi 46, 48

L
La Guma, Alex 35, 40
Land Act 10
Land en Volk (Land and People) 21, 105n
land ownership 98
Langenhoven, CJ 20
languages
  official 101n-102n
Leipoldt, C Louis 20
Leroux, Etienne 51-52
Lewin, Hugh 39, 66
Liberal Party 39
Livingstone, Douglas 66
Lloyd, Lucy 95
Lory, Georges-Marie ix
Luthuli, Albert 64

M
Maeterlinck, Maurice 21
Magona, Sindiwe 84-85
Maimane, Arthur 32
Makana Football Association 4
Makeba, Miriam 58
Malan, Rian 85
Malange, Nise 64, 82
Malay language 16
Manaka, Matsemela 64, 11
Mandela, Nelson 3, 11, 84, 97
Manim, Mannie 60
Maponya, Maishe 64
Marais, Eugène N 21
Market Theatre, The 60

Maseko, Bheki 67-68
Matabele 9
Mathabane, Mark 84
Matshikiza, Todd 58
Matshoba, Mtutuzeli 66
Matthews, James 48
Mbuli, Mzwake 82
McLaren, Robert 63, 113n
Mda, Zakes 65
Medu Art Ensemble 92
Meintjies, Frank 65
Metelerkamp, Joan vii, 97
Mhlophe, Gcina 80
migration 13
Mikro, *see* Kühn, CH
Miller, Ruth 49
Millin, Sarah Gertrude 26
mineworkers 27, 61, 64
missionaries 7
Modisane, Bloke 31, 32-33
Mofolo, Thomas 8-9, 10
Mokoena, Aubrey 82
Motsapi, Seitlhamo 96
Motsitsi, Casey 32
Mphahlele, Ezekiel (later Es'kia) 31-32, 41, 45
Mqhayi, SEK 11-13, 96
Mtshali, Oswald Joseph 46-47
Mtwa, Percy 64, 89
Mutloatse, Mothobe 66

N
Nakasa, Nat 32, 34, 113n
Natal poll tax (1905) 13
National Party 22, 27
Native Land Act (1913) 9-10, 13, 27
Native Trust and Land Act (1936) 27
Ndebele, Njabulo S ix, 66, 76-77, 78-80, 90-91
New Brighton township 62
New Classic, The 113n
New Coin 49, 97
Ngema, Mbongeni 64, 88, 89-90
Nicol, Mike 86
Nkosi Sikelel' i Afrika 11, 103n

Nkosi, Lewis 32-33, 34
Nobel Prize for Literature
　JM Coetzee (2003) 73
　Nadine Gordimer (1991) 73
Nortje, Arthur 43-44, 56
Ntshona, Winston 62
Nxumalo, Henry 'Mr Drum' 32, 34
Nyanga township 57

O
official languages 101-102n
Oliphant, Andries 65, 66
Olympic Games 5
Opperman, DJ 22
Orange Free State 16, 71

P
Pan Africanist Congress (PAC) 2, 3, 39, 84
Paton, Alan 28-29
Pienaar, Lieutenant-Colonel 101n
plaasroman (farm novel) 19, 72
Plaatje, Sol 9-10
Plomer, William 23-24, 25-26
political funerals 80
Poqo 39
Press, Karen 94-95
Prince of Wales 12, 96
Pringle, Thomas 15, 16
prison writing 39
Purkey, Malcolm 88, 90
Purple Renoster, The 69

Q
Qabula, Alfred Temba 64, 82

R
Rabie, Jan 51
Radebe, Dolly 107n
Rammitloa, Marks 107n
Rampolokeng, Lesego 97
Ravan Press 46, 65
Reitz, Deneys 17
Renoster Books 46

Rive, Richard 66
Robben Island 4-5, 43

S

Sabotage Act 39
Sachs, Albie 39
Sampson, Anthony 34
San (/Xam) people 25, 78
Schoeman, Karel 75-76
Schreiner, Olive (Ralph Iron) 17-19, 72
Second World War 27
Sepamla, Sipho 46, 113n
Sepedi 101n
Serote, Mongane Wally 46-48, 66, 71, 77-78, 80, 92-93
Serpent Players 62
Sesotho 101n
Sestigers (Writers of the Sixties) 50-51
Setswana 9, 101n
Shaka 102n
Shakespeare 9
Sharpeville massacre 2-3, 32, 39, 50, 101n
Simon, Barney 60, 64, 89
Siswati 101n
Sitas, Ari 64
S'ketsh' 59, 113n
Slabolepszy, Paul 63, 90
slavery 16
Small, Adam 45-46, 51, 56
Smit, Bartho 36, 51
Smith, Pauline Janet 19-20
Soga, Tiyo 7
Sole, Kelwyn 66, 93
Songololo 117n
Sontonga, Enoch 103n
Sophocles 62
South Africa 6, 22, 44, 58, 82, 87
    apartheid 85
    chaotic transition in 93
    declared a republic 39

democratic 91, 98
  land ownership in 27
  post-civil war 73, 75
  struggle against white rule 8
South African (Anglo Boer) War 1-2
South African Commercial Advertiser 15
South African Communist Party (SACP) 3, 84
South African Journal 15
South African Native National Congress (SANNC) 9
South African War 16-17, 20-21
Soweto uprising/revolt 56, 63-64, 70, 72, 88-89, 104n
Space theatre, The 63
Spanish Civil War 24
Staffrider 65-68, 69
Standpunte (Viewpoints) 21
State of Emergency 39, 81
Stem, Die (The Voice) 21
Stockenström, Wilma 76
strikes 55, 80
Swanson, Donald 107n
Swart, RS Governor-General 2

T
Taalstryd, Die (Struggle for the language) 20
Tambo, Oliver 81
Themba, Can 32, 34
Thomas, Gladys 48
Tlali, Miriam 66
township
  musicals 58
  slang 69
trade-unionism 30
Transvaal Boer republic 17
Treason Trial 32
tricameral parliament (1984) 80
Trotskyists 39
Tshivenda 101n

U
Umqonto we Sizwe 39
Union of South Africa 1
United Democratic Front (UDF) 81

University College of Fort Hare 11
urban employment 27

V
Van den Heever, CM 19
Van der Post, Laurens 25-26
Van Heerden, Etienne 91
Van Wyk, Chris 65, 66-67
Van Wyk Louw, NP 21, 22-23, 51
Van Zyl Slabbert, Frederic 91
Verwoerd, HF 86
Vilakazi, BWB 27-28
Vladislavic, Ivan 65, 86-87
Voorslag (Whiplash) 25
Voortrekkers 22
Vorster, BJ 45

W
Watson, Stephen 95
Wauchope, Rev Isaac (*see also* IWW Citashe) 6-7
white/s 2
    nationalism 22
    poets 49
    population 101n
    writing 14, 36
Wicomb, Zoë 79-80
Willemse, Hein 91
Williams, Pat 58
Winterbach, Ingrid 91
Workshop '71 63

X
Xhosa
    intsomi 65
    language 6-7, 11, 101n
    people 7
    poet 27
Xitsonga 101n
Xuma, Dr AB 107n

Y
Yako, St J Page 27

Z
Zuid-Afrikaansche Republiek of the Transvaal 16
Zulu 46
    language 101n
    king/s 8, 13
Zwelonke, D 39, 40
Zwi, Rose 66
Zwide, K 68-69